WHALE HUNT

"Then, after three quarters of an hour, at the fourth successful blow of the lance, the great responsive lunge of the whale ripped away the harpoon and we lost her. The wind continued to drop. There was almost none. If there had been any, our broken sail would have prevented us from taking good advantage of it. We called in the Kaimoana and set her to the chase, but though the whale was close to exhaustion and hugged the surface, the launch was too slow. We recalled her, and waited for the tow home."

BOOKS BY OLAF RUHEN

Fiction
Land of Dahori
Naked Under Capricorn
The Flockmaster
White Man's Shoes
Lively Ghosts
The Broken Wing

Autobiography
Tangaroa's Godchild

General
Mountains in the Clouds
Minerva Reef
Writing

HARPOON
IN
MY HAND

by
Olaf Ruhen

Originally published in hard cover by
Angus & Robertson, Ltd.

A Tower Natural Heritage Book

HARPOON IN MY HAND

1

"We'll build you a little hut by the beach," said my good friend David Fifita. "We'll make it out of coconut fronds and furnish it Tongan-style, and you can live like Tongans, you and Madeleine. Then in the evenings we'll dance and sing and drink a little kava and all our friends will come; you'll find out what it really means to be a Tongan."

In a dream people say such things; people who swing and sway and change their shapes like seaweed rooted in a racing current; but this was no dream. This was my own house and David at my table.

"We'll build a whale-boat," he went on, this big man, this solid figure in a very real world. "We'll build a whale-boat and when it's finished we'll go whaling. Plenty of good men about. We can get Ha'apai men who know the trade."

He kept on talking, peeling an after-lunch apple for 'Alapasita, his quiet and beautiful wife, who had no English but who needed none, communicating with a supra-normal understanding and quick bright gestures of hands and eyes. I cannot remember what he said next, for I was lost in the fusion of two lifelong fantasies. I have always loved Tonga and the Tongans, and as far back as I can remember I have conned myself into the belief, now fixed, that the concord and sympathy I have felt for whales and their ocean environment amount to yet another kind of love.

When I was a child I lived near a battlement of basalt cliffs that stood against the wild seas ever clawing

5

at a south-eastern coast of New Zealand, far down in the zone of the westerlies and bounding one of the five great migration routes of Antarctic whales. And I would spend some hours of many autumn days nested among the long ripe stalks of cocksfoot that capped the precipice and, sleepy in the sun, would still remain aware of the life about me: the mewing of the gulls, the play of driven water in the rocks below, the breeze rustling the stiff leaves of the veronicas that grew in unplanned hedges all about.

These and the scudding clouds were constant; it was the abnormal that stayed in the memory: the annual visitation of the mutton-birds in their millions, the rare glimpse of a shark in the water far below and, rarer still, the flirted black flag of whale flukes far out to sea, the extrusion of a cask-like head from the surface, or the drifting grey balloons of spoutings.

I would watch these spoutings drift across the crests, excited by them, excited by no more than this: that here in my vicinity a great warm-blooded body passed on its way, serving an intelligence that could circumnavigate the globe without assisting instruments; the master of mariners, prince of the seas, hunted and vulnerable (as every admirable spirit must be vulnerable) but unafraid. My fancy would play with the creator of the small spherical clouds long after the last of each short series had dispersed in the summer air.

Now, as a disbelieving adult, years removed from the pure essence of magic, I am sometimes tempted to think that some of these occurrences were wholly imagined. But not all. I was no more than three or four years of age when I first saw a great flurry of water towards the horizon where, in a fighting frenzy, some agency unimaginably large spooned up the ocean to the sky, and my guardian sister, from the wisdom of her seven or eight years, told me that a sperm was fighting for its life with killer whales.

The information was undoubtedly inaccurate; it would have been no sperm but a humpback on that coast, though we were no more than a leisurely day's whale cruise from the storied Solander Ground which sperms and right whales once haunted in their myriads. It would have been a humpback, but in my extreme youth all large whales were sperms or orcs or rorquals; I didn't know one from another, but the names were intoxicating. As with Samarkand or Petra or Port of Spain, the ectoplasm of adventure was shaken from their sounds.

From time to time I watched such commotions. I am sure now that some were caused by nothing more than the playfulness of whales. Surely most of the whales we saw could not have come inevitably harried by packs of killers. But it is under attack that a whale becomes most conspicuous, and there were times when my eyes could distinguish the narrow peaked banners of the dorsals of the killers, swifter far than their massive quarry, wheeling and doubling against its head.

We may well have missed the more peaceful passages of whales about their more normal occasions; the beast is infrequently obtrusive and cruises out of sight, at most times wholly immersed. There would be small attraction for him at the surface of our wild seas. When his lungs were replenished he would gladly seek the quieter regions below.

What is it that spins an enduring magic from the gossamer of such brief unsatisfactory glimpses? I cannot say, but the thread is powerful still: the whale can still fascinate all the many weak and much-neglected impulses that move me to adventure and the horizon.

Somewhere in the back of my mind I knew that in the kingdom of Tonga, in the Azores, and perhaps in some seas bordering even remoter shores, the whale is still sometimes hunted as it was in the earliest days, with harpoons thrown by hand, with lances wielded from the bows of a small open boat, with sails and oars and such artifacts as any resourceful and inventive man can make with his hands. But David Fifita was the first man I had met who could speak to me with knowledge of the trade, and I was entranced by the possibility that I could participate. In Tonga, so David assured me, the whalers use open boats powered by the wind and sail them, moreover, downwind right to their quarry, thus raising the excitement of the hunt to an even higher pitch than the oarsmen of an earlier century experienced. For the boom hangs wide across the water, the sheet is out to its full extent, the balance is delicate, and the men are divided between their functionally dual duties at the precise moment of contact, when the headsman launches the shaft and the steersman dances like a boxer, anticipating the challenge of the contact joined.

The quarry of the Tongans is mostly the humpback and sometimes the sperm, and they take either whale in the winter months when the south-east monsoon is blowing, in the cold part of the year, from June to October. Sport is not their object, though the Tongan is sportminded, excels at most athletic disciplines, and extracts the utmost enjoyment from encounters with the whale. Nor is any part of the whale diverted to industrial uses. The oil is not saved at all. Each captured whale is an enormous acquisition of protein essential to the Tongan economy, and every digestible scrap of the great body is eaten, along with much that people in richer countries might disdain. The skin, the blubber, and the entrails are eaten with the meat; even the great bones are baked in Tongan earth ovens to draw out the last possible nourishment. There is no waste whatever, and to the Tongan, whose lime-saturated coral soil will produce only limited meat supplies, each whale is a notable prize.

8

Perhaps more important than its material value is the whale's power to make local heroes among those who hunt it. In Tonga it has not yet done this, but the signs are that one day it could. In the fortunate islands of Polynesia the major challenges come, as they always have, from the sea; and the Tongan whalers who hunt, with primitive weapons, the largest and most dangerous animals the world has ever seen are carrying on the traditions of a proud race. In conquering the ocean's greatest hazards they find a confident strength, but, more importantly, their exploits feed the imagination of youth and help to show others that in emergencies men can exceed their normal physical and mental limitations.

Tonga was the centre of a sea-girt empire a thousand years ago, and even today the sea-going Tongan thinks little of setting out on a considerable voyage without a compass or a clock, though he will take them if they are available and he will know how to use them with precision and dispatch.

For a long time before David Fifita extended his casual invitation to adventure I had promised myself that one day I'd go voyaging with Tongans. I could not imagine why this should be different from sailing with other men, but I had a feeling that it would be. My interest in Tonga had developed from the year I turned twelve, when an elder brother had sailed for these Friendly Islands to take over a medical post. In my adolescence I had Tongan mats on my floor and a length of Tongan tapa for my bed. The bark cloth, fawn and brown and black, was the warmest blanket I have ever known, and the lightest. I dreamed of catching my whale, of setting myself and my men against the challenge, of learning through my nerve-ends the crashing crescendo of excitement summoned by a commitment to the struggle. This desire grew strong and solid, and all the persuasions of tolerance and commonsense did

9

not reduce its proportions. I tried to make it an intellectual rather than an emotional necessity, but the effort lacked conviction though I thought my arguments well enough marshalled. I told myself that my interest in whaling was primarily a literary one, and this contained much truth. Much of the unwritten history of European and American penetration of the Pacific was established by the roving whale-ships, and much of the adventure and romance, though they lie buried yet, wait close to the surface for discovery.

A writer's exploitation of such treasure must ideally be accompanied by a knowledge of the emotional reactions of whalers to whaling, of the rhythms by which their life was lived and measured, of the natures of the men engaged and the gamut of their deeds and desires, and of the challenges of their chosen environment.

As if these considerations needed support, David provided additional incentive when he talked of the crew.

"We can get Ha'apai men who know the trade," he said, "but I think we ought to take the survivors of Minerva Reef; they've had plenty of experience and they'll work together. Tevita Uaisele has harpooned nine whales personally and been boat-steerer for three more—he has captained his own boats. Ve'etutu Pahulu has captained boats and captured whales. William Fa knows a lot about it all—we'll have plenty of good men. We can be ready for next whaling season."

It was through Minerva Reef that I had met David. With sixteen companions he had been shipwrecked on that loneliest of South Pacific hazards, and after a hundred and two days of staggering privations, twelve who survived had encompassed their own rescue. David had been their leader, proving himself a man bigger than life-size in every conceivable way. I wrote the story of the tragedy from their accounts and some corroborative evidence; and after he had read my work David became my friend. In this the others joined him.

When I met the survivors first they lay in hospital in a shocking state of malnutrition. David Fifita had lost more than a hundred and twelve pounds in weight. Two of the other men, Finau Laione and William Fa, clung tenaciously to life with puny muscles and mighty wills. The whole twelve were heroes in the best sense of the word, disciplined heroes who had contrived their own deliverance, and I wanted to know more about them. I wanted to see their capacities extended in physical action, since in all humanity they could not be led to further tests of their endurance. I wanted to see them in action against a magnificent and tangible adversary—the whale.

I suppose the vicarious experience—for in writing their story I seemed to live it—had posed questions of an intimate concern to me. Once I had been alone and helpless in an immobilized schooner far from land for three days of a New Zealand storm; on many other occasions I had fought the weather and the waves for several lonely days at a time, once or twice under conditions that seemed to me to press quite dismally upon the normally fragile chances of survival with which man is armoured. I had known cold and loneliness; I had sometimes briefly skirted danger; yet I had never been put to anything like the test that these survivors had triumphantly passed. Could I, in their company, have done what they did? It was and is a rhetorical question. But it was persistent enough to demand action.

All these male joys in the project were supplemented by the excitement of going back to sea, and especially of going in sail. I've always had an attachment to the sea; I am restless when I am not conscious of its great restlessness near by. I can claim to be a man of the sea.

And, finally, it is impossible for a seaman not to be

11

in love with whales; it is impossible for the imaginative man not to vibrate to a contemplated struggle for supremacy with an adversary so vast; it is impossible not to respond to the power and the strength and the loneliness of the kings of the world of waters. The deep disappearances of whales, the songless joy of their great leapings, the unimaginable scope of their wanderings, their capacity for love, their indifference to hate—the whale in his ocean is a challenge to a man.

In mid-June Madeleine and I flew to Tonga. Until we left the tiny airfield of Nausori, outside Suva in Fiji, my excitement had been linked to the excursions of a racing imagination; but from this moment they were kindled and quickened by the physical world that surrounded me. As we edged out from the land over the surrounding reefs, past the yellow water stained by the Rewa River's racing currents, and through the guardian islets of Viti Levu into the freer expanses of the Koro Sea we covered whaling grounds and, a little later, when we raised the Eastern Group and the islands of the Outer Lau, we were over humpback country.

The Koro Sea is a corner of ocean that, as often as I see it, robs me of speech. It is easy to believe that here the creator gods of land and ocean met, here at last conceded their arts to be complementary. Here the islands thrust in a continuing beauty upward from the reef-jewelled deeps to conjure orographic clouds high in the scented air, the clouds in their contribution dappling the sun-flooded lagoons to make their beauty bearable.

Each island is a high hill ringed with a heavy tracery of white surf upon its reefs, as if some chunky green garnet, still uncut, were nesting in a froth of ermine. Its colour is that of the green garnet, a smoky green with its ridged top scabbed with the murkier oxidized tints of the matrix. At the base the frothing surf is separated from each beachy socket, each protruding cape by a rough-trimmed silk of coral lagoon, zircon-green; this enticing calm is fenced from a dancing sea, exquisitely blue, by the ramparts of the reef.

The trades here blow from the south-east; to the north-west of every island, where it affords the most welcome haven to the seaman, each reef is therefore broken by a deep capacious channel scoured by the disciplined waters that daily sweeten the lagoon and its beaches.

Match-sticks of outrigger canoes straked one of the beaches of Matuku, a larger island, and not far from its reef there was a schooner leaning against the wind, a week or more from Suva, perhaps, since the beat was a formidable one against the trades.

Vatoa, half an hour farther on, lay too far to the south to disclose any such signs of human activity; I knew it by repute for a hospitable land where even in the earliest days of European discovery of the Pacific many a shipwrecked mariner was able to shed his throttling fears and regain his full hopes of life. Un-lucky Captain Bligh! Right at the beginning of his long voyage he also passed to the north of it; but he would have feared it, mistrusting its peace. Far to the south of Vatoa I tried my best to distinguish the group of is-lands within a single reef that is Ono-i-Lau, and per-haps I did, or perhaps I saw only a swirl in the horizon mists; I could not tell.

The isolated peoples of most of these islands consti-tute an enclave of Polynesian Tongans among the Me-lanesians of Fiji. Melanesian and Polynesian, dissimilar in everything but dignity and strength, are warm in their friendship for each other and the enclave will never be disturbed; and, if beauty alone has power to hold, they will never leave their houses that are hidden in the cool shade of the forested hills. They have water and life and loveliness, an adequacy of fruits and fish, and a wealth of the flowers and scented leaves that, in

13

the mental balance life achieves there, are even more essential.

But each island stands so lonely that from its shores the next looms only as a smoke-wisp on the horizon, or is altogether out of sight.

Not all of them are inhabited. Quite close to our destination, in the casual estimate of air distances, is Hunga, a necklace of three elements in the north, fair and lovely but inhabited over the centuries only by recluses, fugitives and philosophers, and only then for brief periods. But already we are looking at Tongatapu, lying across the wind like the broken remnant of a great bone fish-hook, twenty miles long and perhaps twelve at its widest. On the side from which we approach, the north-west coast sheltered from the trades, the bay is full of tiny islands, a dozen of them, making a harbour for Nuku'alofa, the capital. Complexities of reef make the harbour a difficult one; the changing depths produce a mosaic of contrasting colours.

Right against the shore are the red roofs of the palace and its chapel, and round about, scattered with an easy carelessness, the buildings of the town. But the airfield lies on the windward side of the island and we glided there, losing height over a land that from the air is disappointing and belies its true character by looking unattractive. The coconut plantations that cover most of it are too old; too many of the palms are gaunt and ragged with age or the overenthusiastic harvesting of the useful leaves. The land itself is flat or so gently tilted that few natural features draw the eye, except about the centre of the island where the inroads of the sea have formed shallow harbours of considerable quiet beauty, and on the south-west coast, where for mile after mile the heaving ocean is spasmodically fountained through blow-holes in the coral to create a never-ending spectacular of patterned water that beads the air with brief diamonds.

As our aircraft continued to lose height the impression of a remembered loveliness returned with the sight of the coco-leaf houses grouped in helter-skelter villages where racing bands of playing children seemed bright as the ever-present flowers. Neat swept lawns. Impressionistic hedges that indicated boundaries without barring the way. Roads where carts drawn by jogging horses coped with a heavy foot traffic. Clearings where taro sprouted its velvet leaves higher than a man, or small green banana cuttings starred the red-brown soil with green. Plantations with an even crop of the paper mulberry, or, remote from roads where they would draw attention, shrubberies of treasured kava identifiable by the heart-shaped leaves. And then we were bouncing over the rough tropic grass of a Tongan field.

Our friends waited not at all for the formalities of Customs and Immigration. David and his wife 'Ala, heading a squadron forty strong, advanced across the field the moment the aircraft door was opened, to press their cheeks to ours in greeting and to load our necks with *Kahoas*, which are a little different from Hawaiian leis, and our waists with *sisis*, which are unlike any other garlands I know. Fresh and fragrant, they loaded the air with perfume and were soft as a lover's lips to the accidental touch. Hands reached for our luggage, others capped us with party hats newly woven from cream-green coco-leaves just unfurled, musicians struck up their guitars and singers broke into a song of welcome written for the occasion, and, from the hosts of beautiful children, individuals, shy but happy, came forward with a diffident greeting. The waiting officials rose to the occasion and stamped our documents with a minimum of formality and a maximum of flourish, while our fellow passengers watched in a mild bewilderment. We piled into a chartered bus, and the musicians, still playing, put in an early claim for the front seats where their instruments could be relatively playable. As driver Teiapa'a let out the clutch and the bus rocked towards the road, a mother pushed her small child into the aisle to dance for us while we travelled.

Child after child joined this impromptu chorus, none of them disconcerted by the rocking of the bus, which indeed was not excessive, for Teiapa'a was careful to stay well within the twenty-mile-an-hour speed limit (five miles at intersections) necessitated by the crowded foot traffic of the roads. But when the dancers, not all of them children, lurched off balance, the immediate reaction was a shout of laughter. We made a rowdy progress towards the capital.

On the outskirts the bus slowed to a crawl while people pointed out our house. But we did not disembark, beginning instead a triumphal tour of Nuku'alofa, up each street and down the next, past the Parliament and the palace and finally along the waterfront. Here we paused briefly where a stone pier ran out over the coastal reef to deep water, and at its root, lying on the green grass, a white whaler rested on her side, the name *Velata* painted big and black against her lovely bows, her interior timbers red-leaded—a joy of weathered red—her mast and rudder gone. The pause was momentary, the laughing and the singing too loud to permit of clear explanations, but I knew that she was ours; and knew too that she was good.

When we had covered every street of the town Teiapa'a brought us back at last to our house. Its walls and roof were formed from 1440 plaited coconut fronds; the number was accurately known, for in a changing tropics the fronds may no longer be gathered for nothing in such population centres as Nuku'alofa but are bought for three-pence each. They were still fresh and bright green, though had the house been intended to last beyond the few months of our occupancy they would have been carefully weathered to a rich brown.

Our hosts had not finished the building until early that same morning; they had worked night and day to prepare for us.

When I stepped inside it was cool and comfortable. It did not seem strange but had an aura of friendliness such as surrounds a house good for living. Fresh flowers were everywhere; the walls and ceiling were studded with blazing hibiscus blossoms and the quieter loveliness of lilies. But at that moment I did not realize how much I would come to love this place.

The music stopped briefly during the indispensable drinking of kava and then resumed while we dealt with the first of our Tongan feasts, a noble offering of three or four spit-roasted pigs, quantities of chickens and fish baked in coconut milk in an earth oven, mangrove crabs and crayfish brilliant red on the fresh green ten-foot trays of coconut frond with banana-leaf tray-cloths, breadfruit in several guises, bananas and watermelons and young coconuts for drinking.

The house was crowded then, and was often crowded after, but it was an ample dwelling. Above the low walls on three sides a three-foot opening was provided with plaited coconut-leaf blinds, and on the fourth side a bedroom had been walled off. This was completely lined with richly patterned tapa cloth, as were the upper walls and ceiling of the outer room. The floors were inches deep in fine hand-woven mats. The Tongan bed was a foot-deep mound of mats and tapa, nine feet square. A table, two stools and a bench, and a cupboard for foodstuffs were concessions to European idiosyncrasy. The cupboard's content included knives, forks, and spoons, plates, cups, and saucers. Otherwise we were to live as the Tongans do.

Fakapulia, a heavy silent man, was our guard. He dressed in the Tongan style, in the *vala*, with bare legs. Everything about him was correct, for he was a *matapulei,* one of the appointed—as distinct from the he-

17

reditary—noblemen of Tonga. Since his was a royal appointment he must always be dressed in Tongan style, but he would have done this anyway for our arrival. From the moment we entered the house he sat stiffly, watching our needs. Correctly, he stayed seated every moment I was present, keeping his head below the level of mine.

Fakapulia adhered closely to the conventions, and from that time took what seemed almost an avuncular interest in my movements. He was officially on duty at our house for one day only, but we were never without a guard the whole time we were in Tonga. The guard was our lock and key; he watched over our possessions. He was our message-boy and tried to anticipate our needs. He was our directory and information bureau; he saw everything without seeming to look. On days subsequent to our first he was one of our crew, usually Ve'etutu Pahulu; but if Ve'etutu had to leave the house temporarily, Finau Laione or one of the others would relieve him.

When in later weeks I was away at sea, these men in unobtrusive attendance were as unobtrusively replaced by women, to guard Madeleine. And at all times the house was headquarters for troops of children, laughing and playing, dancing and singing, subconsciously learning a perfection in natural hospitality.

Against this background it might have been easy to forget our mission, but my necessity to catch a whale was urgent and ever-present; among people less balanced than these it might easily have grown into an obsession. But our hosts, too, needed the catch; beneath the singing and the laughter the conversation cleaved to the same topic always, the whale and whaling, the quarry and the chase, the men, the gear and the beautiful white hull of the whaler, designed to a single purpose and glorious in her propriety to that end.

18

2

The music, the dancing, and the drinking of kava that celebrated our arrival went on with undiminished intensity until midnight precisely, when it stopped, making way for the Sabbath. In no time at all the guests had gone, the onlookers had dispersed, and we had retired to the privacy of our room. I fell asleep immediately, drained by the release of contained excitement; but in three hours or so I awoke, to lie and think of ships and whales and voyages. It would have been difficult to turn my thoughts elsewhere, for it is a sea air that invests the scented islands in their dark still nights, an air unmistakably of ocean, lively and salt-bearing and rippled with meaningful sound.

In the city life that most of us have come to accept as normal, the noises that beset the tired man in his bed will bring discomfort, jar his sleep, and probably spoil his morrow; but the night sounds of Tonga are enchanted confirmation of the security and peace that is darkness; they are the warranty of continuing bright and busy life, evidence of the link between man and his appropriate surroundings.

If no storm threatens, the most persistent night

sound is the call of the *fuleheu*, a small honeyeater with a loud, wide-ranging voice, a musical talent, and an irrepressible excitement inevitably evoked by the promise of a sunny day to come.

The *fuleheu* sings and waits and is answered, and sings again and persists in his calling until all his friends and relations seem to have responded, and then subsides, for never more than half an hour or so. He is earlier and more persistent than the village cocks, but they too are ubiquitous in the island world; and the cocks will raise their voices whether the day to come be promised fair or foul. Cocks and honeyeaters rouse up a tuneful cricket with a thin and reedy voice; and none of these is silenced even when the *ata-'a-puaka*, the "dawn of pigs" arrives, and the swine begin their restless search for a non-existent superfluity, the dogs make indignant protest, and good men stretch contentedly beside their wives, composing themselves for the last sweet hour of sleep.

Not all of them; for with the *ata-'a-puaka*, and long before the light, the throbbing of the *lalis* begins, calling the faithful of several sects to their first worship of the day. Each *lali* is a deep-troughed tree trunk lying on the ground, its open top protected from the rain by a thatched roof. It is raised on pillars so that the drummer rarely has to stoop; he stands and swings his mallet at the *lali's* edge, calling up deep notes that lose but little strength across the miles. In Tonga the faithful advertize their state; when heads are counted publicly the tally of the uncommitted sinners is a paltry one, and an incessancy of ringing church-bells and shivering, throbbing *lalis* triumphantly proclaims the condition of the converted. It is almost sad that in the night of sound even such insistent remembrancers are all too easily overlooked.

I have loved night sounds in many places. In the city where I live my home is situated so fortunately that I can hear the loons and the boobook owls in early morning, and the traffic hardly at all. And through my first nights in Tonga a joy of orientation kept me from sleep. I never complain of wakefulness. If sleep is necessary nature provides it; if it is remote there is never a monotony in the world of consciousness. So on this first night, as on many nights to come, I lay relaxed upon the pile of mats that was as hard and as restful as a bed upon the earth itself, and let my unfamiliarity make conscious work of isolating each characteristic sound.

And in the night young Finau Laione Sekona, the youngest of the survivors from Minerva Reef, sleeping with the rest of our guard in the ante-room, called piteously, almost frantically, in his sleep:

"Don't steal my water. Don't take my water. Leave it alone and let me keep it."

His companions heard him and felt the rough male tenderness of protectors. The shipwreck was nearly two years behind Finau and he was young, not yet twenty; but for the rest of his life he would be unable to prevent himself from showing signs of the sufferings it had imposed upon him. The even tenor of his developing life had been shattered by the disaster in his eighteenth year when he was yearning for manhood but still remained a child, when consciously he acted like a brave and indeed a noble man and subconsciously reacted like a child, when he had been proud to give an example to the world he was yet too young to know.

No germs of illness could survive on Minerva Reef. A reasonably healthy man marooned there could console himself with the certainty that, whatever disaster might befall him—and there was a considerable choice —he could not catch a cold. The ancestors of the Tongans shipwrecked there had come in ages past to islands with air as salubrious, where disease germs did not exist and where no maladies developed until they were introduced by other voyagers a score of centuries later. There was little wonder that, in the early days of European contact when Polynesians were laid low by new germs to which they proved most vulnerable, they sometimes attributed their sorry condition to a malevolent witchcraft. They were not far wrong.

Finau, sailing to New Zealand with the *Tuaikaepau*, had been bright and active, apparently in the best of health; but under his skin he must have carried the germs of tuberculosis. The enforced inaction for three and a half months on the wreck, the inadequate diet and clothing, and the dubious shelter on the coldest and most southerly of coral reefs lowered his resistance. The germs flourished, so that physically he wasted away more than, and more quickly than, the others. He was naturally small, and he became so thin he seemed certain to die; it was ridiculous that existence, let alone exuberance, should persist within that emaciated frame. But Finau had no thought of dying, and his courage carried him through; other men lay dead while he still had no thought of anything but a crowded and abundant future. Whenever the receding tide made it possible he ran about on the drying reef like a ghost crab on the sand; never still, never despondent, always on the lookout: even capable at times of finding things to laugh at in the problems that beset the company. When there were tasks to be done he was always at Captain David's elbow, eager to be allotted his share of duties. At other times he got into mischief, like a child.

"Finau is to come whaling, but he's to have no work to do," David had stipulated. "He's to have a place in the boat, but he can just work if he wants to. No one is to give him orders. Wherever I go, whatever I do, there will always be a place for him."

Finau's deceased grandmother on his mother's side was a European who, many years before, had left a job in the Burns Philp store in Vava'u to marry a Tongan.

22

She abandoned the English language with other characteristics of her earlier life. Her children, when they grew, spoke nothing but Tongan, but they had fair straight hair, and sharp European features, firm and set, as though they came from barren lands, as though they belonged to Scotland or Vermont among the heather or the paintbrush flowers. They passed these characteristics on to Finau's generation, though the females reflected them more vividly than the males. Yet they were Tongan, wedded to the customs and the language of the country. They had no yearnings to find out much or anything about their European relatives. Only their features were alien in their islands, and perhaps a certain slightness of build, for they looked less sturdy than Tongans of a purely Polynesian ancestry (though Finau proved their resilience).

The other survivors, sleeping in our ante-room, would hear the cry for water in the night, and would be especially tender with Finau next morning, for the dream came more than once.

That first night we hardly knew who else was in the house with us. Our homestead swarmed with girls. David Fifita was the father of a son and seven daughters, of whom five permanently and one temporarily still lived at home. Pina, the eldest, lived with her husband and children in a village a few miles away on the same island; she was a frequent visitor. Senituli was also married, but was currently absent from her home on an island in the Ha'apai group and was visiting her parents. At the energetic centre of domestic activity were three teenaged schoolgirls, Stella, Tokilupe, and Virginia. Not yet in their teens were Paea and Eneio.

The names were musical, delightful indeed, but most of them were not easy for Europeans to take in at first. Senituli, big with her third child, remarkable for her enormous, soft, expressive eyes, was a beautiful girl, not easy to forget; her name was difficult until we realized it was an English one—Century; for she had been born on the hundredth anniversary of the Roman Catholic Church in Tonga.

There are only sixteen letters in the Tongan alphabet, and consonants are never placed together. "Sitela" was thus the island form of "Stella" and was pronounced the same. As a rule, but not consistently, Stella adopted the English form when she wrote anything for us. Tokilupe, beautiful too—they were all beautiful, all seven of the girls—had a name that meant nothing much, in either English or Tongan. Visinia—that was Virginia. It was her confirmation name; her given name, which she used exclusively when writing, was Faka'ilokimoana, of which the translation is "Report from the Deep Ocean". Paea was born immediately after her grandfather's death by drowning; her full name was Paea-i-vaha, "orphaned by the deep". And Eneio was named for a *liku*, a place on the cliffs of the Vava'u group much frequented by lovers. In her name-place, when the moon is right, its light so shines upon a play of the tides in the narrow channels beneath as to give the effect of a woman swimming; it is a romantic place in the romantic islands.

Names come in a fantastic variety in Tonga, for they are given by aunts, and a Tongan aunt is formidable. A suggestion from royalty or the nobility may override the wishes of aunts, but this happens seldom. Sometimes it seems almost that Tongan aunts wish to be remembered for their inventiveness; but however unusual the names turned out to be, they were borne lightly. Paea's "orphaned by the deep" did not worry her cheerful little head at all; in the same house was a child named for the death of Paea's eldest brother Sateki, a boy who drowned in a gallant attempt to save the remaining castaways on Minerva Reef. To this remembrance she carried the name Apokivaha, "to Death from the Deeps". She was a beautiful child, then two

24

years old, with the smiles of angels in her lively features, though she was marred by a deformity of the ankles which made it probable that she would never walk upright.

David shared a large house, the one-time Nuku'alofa Yacht Club, with his lifelong friend Sioeli Kaho, who had also sired a family of nine that was reduced by the death of one member to seven girls and a boy, of more or less the same ages as the Fifita children.

When we held a quiet court that Sunday the problems called up by all the strange names seemed never-ending, but as far as I was concerned they were getting only secondary consideration. I was busy reconciling myself with the exasperation of a Tongan Sunday on which no one can work, even to tinker with a boat. An extract from Tonga's written constitution runs: "The Sabbath Day shall be sacred in Tonga forever, and it shall not be lawful to do work or play games or trade on the Sabbath. And any agreement made or document witnessed on this day shall be counted void, and shall not be recognized by the Government."

But every aspect of the life about us was full of interest, and since members of the Fifita and Kaho families were all Roman Catholics Sunday was something less of a trial than it might have been in stricter Wesleyan circles. The only working activity, nevertheless, was the cooking of meals, for which the materials had all been gathered on the day before.

All the land worships on Tonga's Sunday. There are no dissenters. Even the Seventh Day Adventists, who normally go to church on Saturday, find themselves in line with the rest of the land because of an inflexible attitude to the International Date Line and perhaps also because of the consideration that Tonga's Sunday Observance laws would impose two Sabbaths in every week for those who keep Saturday holy. Fabric of bells and *lalis* shudders throughout the day, the sweet and

25

vibrant protests saturate the sunshine. Processions of worshippers, barefooted and parasoled and dressed in their best, make a never-ending pilgrimage from house to church and back again.

When on that first day we felt the movement envelop us David the Catholic took us to the fiercely Protestant service of the Methodists. This was partly in deference to our own beliefs but chiefly because of the music; all the sects delighted in their sacred songs and all of them were excellent, but those of the Methodists in their enormous church drew a huge congregation.

We had chosen better than we knew. A new Conference of the Methodist Church was about to be established in the South Pacific, which thus would become a newly autonomous area, no longer looking to Australia for direction. To mark the relinquishment of control, the President-General of the Methodist Church in Australasia, Dr. W. F. Hambly, with other high-ranking officials, was spending this week in Tonga and not one but fourteen choirs, singing in unison and independently, supported the evening church service. As each choir finished its offering and sat down, another stood up; when the front-rank choirs had all contributed, those farther back stood up, the conductor balancing himself among the silent singers on the front benches.

The Queen's choir was supported by a strong brass section. All the others sang without accompaniment, but with their glorious component voices tempered to a magnificent proportion. Many of the great doors that intersected the church walls at frequent intervals were open; but the voices sounded as though they could have filled the great outdoors. The singers were so highly trained it seemed incredible that hardly any of them, choristers or conductors, could read music; their vocal efforts were daring, and never transgressed a true relationship.

26

The women of the choirs all dressed in white. The men, too, wore white shirts and neat white *valas*, in which I never saw them without reflecting that the knee-length skirt is essentially a masculine garment; no woman can wear it with the authority and dignity of a man.

Some of the choristers were barefooted, most of them wore open thong sandals. Most of the women carried fans, beautifully fashioned from pandanus strips or the protective sheath of the coconut flower, and constantly in motion. Shod or not, all were accounted well dressed, for they wore the *ta'ovala*, a cincture of matting, embroidery or some other work without which, indeed, they would have been regarded as shameless, as though they had come to church naked.

Strangely enough, the women were mainly hatless, even the European visitors. To go hatless was, of course, more comfortable, but comfort has scant influence on Tongan dressing, which normally goes to superfluous lengths. But there is in the Methodist church in Tonga a system whereby the right to wear a hat to church is conferred upon regular churchgoers who pass an examination in the Scriptures. Thereafter they are known as *akonaki,* the instructors, and are recognized as leaders—as being capable, for example, of teaching religion. These jealously guard their privilege of covering their heads in church, but, even so, reserve it for special occasions.

The church service, which began at 7.30 p.m. continued for more than three hours, and I became restless only during the brief periods in which the several speakers had their say. I have seldom been long held or much impressed by religious services, but as an onlooker here I could identify my own vague searchings for an infinite truth with the pride and the glory and the frank and wholesome adoration that soared on the voices to the star-lamped skies.

3

We had originally planned to build a whaler with the materials available in Tonga, equip it with gear of our own manufacture, and thus go to sea like true primitives, just men against the whale. This we could have done; indeed, given the combined skills of our team, we could even have laid up our ropes, woven our own sails, pitsawn our own timber. But time was too short, the start of the whaling season was too near, and since we could not make our sun stand still, we chose to make him run.

In the month before my arrival David had acquired the use of *Velata*, rather lengthier than most Tongan whalers at 32 feet, and beamier at 8 feet 6 inches, yet an obvious delight to any seaman's eye. And to any lubber's, for that matter. No one of feeling can be blinded to true excellence by mere technical ignorance. But the man with an involvement is positive in his response; the sweet clean vibrant lines that delight us in the tyrannies of the ships and the horses and the women that we tame have a quintessential beauty. Ships and horses and women, birds and aircraft: living beings and nearly living artifacts that, like abstract notions, can command a sacrifice of lives or days.

I could have been in love with *Velata*. I often think I was. Nor is this a perversion of love, for the sirens lived, and men created them.

Her careenage, by the foot of the Yellow Pier, was about a quarter of a mile from the Overseas Wharf and Nuku'alofa centre. She was stripped down to a skin that, on an inspection closer than the bus had afforded, was scabrous with old paint and handling scars. The temporary expedients of desperate men had overlaid her with cheap and unnecessary timber patches, but her fundamental beauty was of the kind that cannot be marred. When I saw her I tried in my mind's eye to put her into contest with the whale—for I had to see her as an ally and not a tool—and as nearly as I could judge she was adequate. That was a superlative in commendations, for I had a hungry eye for faults.

The job that faced us amounted to a rebuilding. All her ribs had to be duplicated, eight heavy frames reinforced with boiler-plate were to strengthen her bottom and hold her to shape, new naturals were to strengthen her bottom and hold her to shape, new naturals were to hold her thwarts and centre-board box, the loggerhead was to be reset, and decks installed forward for harpooner and hunting gear, aft for steersman and line-tubs—four decks in all. Gratings had to protect the rest of the bottom. Cleats had to take the place of a horse for the sheet. A new capping, with new rollock bases, would form a gunwale. Some planks had to be replaced, nearly all the caulking renewed.

There were gaps you could see through, some of them at the water level and below. The putty was cracked and falling from the seams, and there were some well-developed whiskers of old caulking shaking in the trade wind.

But the name *Velata* was spread across the bows

with a fine large flourish and a dignity not quite compatible with the brush-marks of red lead and tar that splashed the crusty white exterior and the orange innards. She was ragged and holed, and any man not of the sea might have believed she had been pulled up on the bank for a final disposal. Even a seaman might have left her there; and she had been lying on a similar bank in Ha'apai when David first sighted her.

Negotiation with the owner secured her for nothing, though her reputation was as sweet as her lines. For one reason, Ha'apai men stick together. For another, there would be an ample hire in the value of the repairs necessary to maintain her in the water for a season. For a third, there had been no other bidder in the market.

With three crewmen and his twelve-year-old son Fifita, David went to Ha'apai to collect her. Storm winds from the height of the wet monsoon were ruling the weather, and he was delighted that one other sailing-boat wanted to make the eighty-mile passage to Nuku'alofa. He had no great hope that *Velata* would stay in one piece and his only comfort, strangely, was financial—the arrangement with the owner specified that should she break up or be lost David would carry no liability. When they launched the boat the storm increased. But there could be no delay; *Velata* could have sunk at her moorings at any time, and if this had happened we would have lost the chance of a whale-boat altogether, and our plans, for that season anyway, would have come to nothing. No other possible boat was available.

David persuaded the crew of the companion vessel to up-anchor and ride down the storm, a proceeding about which they were highly doubtful. But they too appreciated company, for they were an inexperienced crew and not conversant with the gantlet of reefs between Ha'apai and the capital.

With this insurance David and his crew set out.

Under the driving pressures of her sail *Velata's* leaks increased. Three men armed with four-gallon cans bailed her constantly, and still the incoming water kept pace with their efforts.

As she lay over from the wind a new series of holes opened just above the normal waterline. Young Fifita, his face shining with delight, his legs carrying him at the run over the gunwale cap in preference to the obstacle race of the thwarts, ripped off his small shirt and stuffed it into the worst of the holes, and then sought rags and scraps of what material lay available to make temporary running repairs at the other cracks and holes.

David, who has a passion for mathematics in any form, watched the men and calculated that, in the eight hours of their racing passage, they threw one hundred and seventy-three tons of water over the side. Yet more came in; they reached the beach at Nuku'alofa wading more than knee-deep in the shallow vessel and almost exhausted from the bailing.

The endurance of the Tongan is so frequently called upon to compensate for the absence of proper gear that such a sustained effort as this evokes little island comment other than a friendly and admiring badinage. But nothing could have dampened the crew's delight, not only in the safety of landfall, but also in the convincing evidence of *Velata's* potential as a fast, lively vessel. With her hull half full and wallowing in heavy seas, the greater part of her unwanted cargo must have come in over the rail, but the little sloop, heavy and unresponsive as she must have been, kept company with her companion to the end.

That delivery crew, with other men intended for the permanent crew, gathered on the beach ready to begin the repairs. Not all of them were survivors from Minerva Reef. David had tried to ensure that they would be, but some of the survivors were in other islands or

New Zealand and not all were suitable. There was Talo, for example, David's illegitimate son who, through his long ordeal on the reef had taken with increasing resentment the recriminations of other survivors who blamed him for the whole disaster of the wreck, since his had been the hand at the wheel in the moment of impact. Talo was not to remain with us for very long. He had, in the mildest of forms, some of the qualities of the agitator. In other words, he pressed for rewards for his services, and as soon as David became aware of this, Talo was sent back to the farm.

There was Finau Laione, willing and deft, but inexperienced. He spent much of his time helping Ve'etutu to guard our house and some of the rest running messages.

Fine Feuiaki, clever with his hands and a good engineer, seemed to work from morning till night without complaint. We saw little, however, of Teiapa'a Bloomfield, a taxi-driver who, incredibly, had never learned to swim until he forced himself to it in the loneliness and the danger of Minerva Reef. Teiapa'a was officially of our number; he had indeed conceived such a great admiration for David in their deliverance from the reef that he wanted to follow him everywhere.

In the tensions of life on the reef Teiapa'a gathered from the dreams of an encroaching madness a resolution to kill Fine Feuiaki. David by this time, had left, seeking rescue in his tiny boat, and Fine spent all his days crouched over the fire, trying to distil water. Teiapa'a, convinced that Fine was helping himself to more than his share—as in the last two days Fine undoubtedly was—had decided to kill him in the night, and had selected his weapon, and was waiting for the small hours of morning for his chance. "Teiapa'a" means "a road cut into the steep side of a hill", and Teiapa'a Bloomfield walked a narrow track that night and teetered above a frightful precipice. But at midnight came

32

the sound of the rescuing aircraft. Plots were forgotten, and madness banished.

Teiapa'a and Fine were now the best of friends. Fine was well aware of what Pa'a's intentions had been, and it was a tribute to both of them that no embarrassment existed on this score. Indeed it often provided material for cross-banter. To a more sophisticated mind than the Tongan's, embarrassment would seem the least of the potential consequences of a frustrated murder plot.

Teiapa'a's father was having a busy season with his buses, trucks, taxis, and hire tractors. He was, moreover, confined to hospital with an ailing heart, and since his son had recovered miraculously from his misadventure at sea, he wanted him to stay ashore and attend to driving. Teiapa'a had a dread of offending his father. He had done so once before, at the time of his embarkation on the disastrous voyage, and while he wanted to remain with David through the whaling season he hoped to comply with his father's wishes in everything else. He compromised by shouldering all our transportation worries in the intervals of dashing about with bus or taxi. He was able to do this more readily because in Tonga buses have routes but no schedules. They are apt to run when the driver estimates that enough passengers will be waiting. We were returning home from a picnic once, in a taxi driven by Teiapa'a, when he noticed large numbers of schoolboys waiting for the bus that would drive them to their dormitories after a weekend at home. The bus served districts farther out than the school, but Pa'a's mouth watered at the rich pickings here. He raced back to the garage, got out a bus, and ran a special service to the school, collecting a sum that probably represented the cream of the profit for the man who owned the route. The rank individualism reflected by this behaviour adds no little to the unpredictable charm of life in Tonga.

The most valuable man in the crew was Tevita Uaisele. In a modern community he would probably become a leader, a member of the knees-and-elbows aristocracy. In Tonga, though he was still young, his record was remarkable. A Ha'apai man, he had been bred to the sea and apprenticed to a boat-builder. He neglected neither avenue. He had been harpooner or boat-steerer for a dozen captured whales, and he had built many boats. From the latter trade he had launched out and developed a small business in house-building—small only because Tongan opportunities are so limited.

Though he had no English, Tevita had seized what chances he could of visiting New Zealand, where his habit was to work for a boat-builder in Auckland. He was so appreciated that the language difficulty did not become a barrier. Though he and the manager spoke no common tongue and neither had an interpreter, blueprints were a universal guide. Tevita had only to be shown one to follow it; as soon as he knew what was required of him he went ahead with the job. Since he had no English he had no small-talk, and never kept another man off the job. He could not be flurried or flustered, and he never watched a clock.

To Tevita Uaisele, working in "civilization" was an eye-opener. He had never had it so easy; for the Polynesian, who is often described as "lazy" by the European living in the islands as well as by the tourist, is a devoted and intelligent worker. While in New Zealand, Tevita would live on the cargo of roots carried by whatever schooner had taken him there, or on the hospitality of resident Tongans. Every penny he made could be saved.

On his return to Tonga, then, he became a man of some consequence. He had tools, well-kept; this was the basis of a fortune in the islands where good tools are above prize. He rode a motor-cycle of a fairly modern vintage; this helped him to order his days efficiently. As time went on he had several jobs, with men employed on each one. He could play as hard as he worked. Sometimes, when he had something to celebrate, he would do so on Australian beer in the Tonga Club. When this happened, Teiapa'a, an ex-toper who had sworn off European beer and spirits because of his deliverance from Minerva Reef, would first remove Tevita's bike from the club precincts and whatever loose money he could extract, with skill or guile, from Tevita's pockets; and then, after disappearing for an interval he deemed sufficient for sustained celebration, would return to the club for Tevita's person and take it home to its rightful bed.

On Minerva Reef, Tevita Uaisele and another of our crew, William Fa, had been the carpenters who contrived a rescue craft from the timbers of a wreck where they had all found shelter. They had for tools only a table-knife, a hammer, and a chisel-ended nail, and because of this poverty, and because they were expert, they delegated little of the work. When it was over William Fa collapsed completely, but Tevita went on to undertake, with David and David's doomed son Sateki, the extended ordeal of an open-boat voyage, without rations and without shelter, four hundred miles to Fiji: eight hard days at sea in which his most effective sustenance came from the shared blood of a little seagull thinned with the spirits from the boat-compass.

Tevita was steady, quiet-spoken, dependable. If that were all he might have been no more than a straw-boss. But, like most of his people, he also has a touch of the poet in him; and I say that he therefore has the constituent qualities of a leader.

Maile Siakumi had had no direct connection with Minerva Reef, but he was a key man in the whaling crew. By hard work he had, earlier in life, achieved ownership of *Vaisingano*, a fine whaling vessel built, and truly built, by Tevita Uaisele. In mid-September of

1962, while Tevita and the others were on Minerva Reef and most people believed them dead, three lads stole Maile's boat. They headed for America, struck storm, and were rescued by a fishing vessel which, in subsequent difficulties, had to cast *Vaisingano* adrift. It was never seen again.

Though in this moment the tangible product of Maile's working life was destroyed, along with his future chances, he took the blow with dignity and an outward calm. He had loved *Vaisingano*, and she had offered him the opportunity of leading the kind of life he liked most; but there were no recriminations. Maile was a decided acquisition to our company.

Lau'ia Kilifi was also of our crew, one of the leaders; but at this early stage I saw little of him for a reason that illuminated a part of his character. Since the whaling regulations of Tonga required that any boat engaged in the chase should be accompanied by another vessel capable of rescuing the crew of the first should it be smashed by the whale or otherwise destroyed, David Fifita had also acquired a launch, named *Kaimoana*. She was a round-bottomed rolling witch, incapable of carrying sail, and powered by an obstreperous diesel which, when it was efficient, pushed her along at about three and a half knots. But like *Velata* she had cost us little. She belonged to a distant relation of David's, and the arrangement was that should we catch whales we could pay for her hire whatever amount we believed it to be worth. Incidentally we could make a few repairs, such as replacing a rudder almost completely eaten away by electrolytic action. Since it was a mild-steel rudder with copper fastenings it could not have lasted more than a year or two at the outside, and because we were limited to the same materials, neither could our replacement.

When Lau'ia came into the crew David asked him to act as watchman on *Kaimoana*, which was moored in a

36

small boat harbour named Fa'ua; and from this post Lau'ia never stepped ashore, though the distance was about six feet. He often went without food when the rest of the crew forgot to supply him; but not even a hunger of several day's duration would induce him to leave his charge unguarded. Unless *Kaimoana* was at sea or he could get a reliable replacement, he was sure to be found in *Kaimoana's* long cabin (she had been a ferry in one of the New Zealand fiords).

Of middle height, Lau'ia was of Adonis proportions. He was deep-chested and well-muscled. His expression was unchangingly pleasant; but his greatest quality was his capacity for a regimented endurance. When the whaling began he stood on *Velata's* lively rail for hours at a stretch, day after day, and was normally the first to sight a whale.

His rare relief on *Kaimoana* was likely to come in the person of Molimoli Finau. Molimoli was thin and dark and wore earrings, but was far from effeminate. For that matter, all the tough whaling men could wear flowers in their hair and carry little decorated handbags to hold their money and their cigarettes, and occasionally scent themselves without loss of dignity or male status. Because of their poverty they sometimes found it necessary to wear a woman's dress when they went to sea or engaged in some of the rougher, dirtier tasks on shore, thus keeping their few clothes good. Tongan law provides the huge penalty of a ten-pound fine for any man who appears on a public street without a shirt. Eight pounds is a month's wages, so Tongans seldom transgress. But crew members of visiting ships now and again contribute to Tongan coffers in this way.

It was some time before I was on familiar terms with all the members of the crew. Some were so retiring that in the beginning I did not always distinguish them from the crowd of casual helpers and onlookers who attended us. But Sioeli Kaho was always outstanding. His full

37

grey beard and his wild shock of hair sprouted from a face of great character, a Polynesian face but one that would have caused no surprise at all in America's New England, a hard and ruggedly handsome face lighted with eyes of understanding.

In Tonga there is not much opportunity for the practitioners of any arts save music and dancing; Sioeli's interest in these was sincere, perhaps as proof of which he had married Ana-Malia, the most notable danseuse Tonga had seen in generations. He showed no other interest in the prime arts, but essentially his nature was creative. In a land where opportunities were more varied and flexible he would probably have been a writer. He had a deep regard for history, he loved to emphasize the cogent detail, and he had a memory that specialized in the colours of contact.

He had been a lifelong friend of David's. They had gone to school together in Ha'apai and then, as they entered their teens, they went together to the same school in Nuku'alofa. From this they were both expelled, in the same month and for the same reason: each, in spite of his tender years, had got a girl pregnant and cheerfully admitted it. After more than thirty years each took a strong personal interest in this offspring of his early teens.

That was during the world-wide depression of the thirties. Tonga, a one-crop country, suffered badly. David, with his father a sea-captain and his future committed to the ocean, had no difficulty in entering the kind of life he wanted. Sioeli had none either, but his desires were far from conventional. He studied gambling and became a poker-player of no mean order. Though in Tonga the opportunities seemed limited, he retained enough from his winnings to marry Ana-Malia, raise a family, and avoid conventional work for a lifetime. He also kept enough money to indulge to noble proportions a taste for *kava papalangi,* the white man's liquors—any of them: beer, whisky, rum, gin, wine, or brandy.

The only work he loved was fishing. Whenever there was a place on a boat he would go to sea, particularly if the destination was the deep-sea drift grounds thirty or forty miles offshore. He would undergo severe discomforts for the chance of the game, and if the luck proved bad he would stay out for days without food or rest.

Sioeli's unusual achievement was to combine the happy status of a bum with a position in which he commanded the considerable respect of most of the community. At first sight this was difficult to understand. He certainly had a talented wife; while we worked on the boat an advanced student of anthropology connected with the Bishop Museum in Hawaii came to Tonga to study Polynesian dancing under Ana-Malia for her doctorate thesis. Though Ana-Malia was in her fifties she could dance with an exquisite controlled abandon that raised her fans to delirious heights of appreciation. And Tu'imala, their eldest daughter, was a favourite of Queen Salote; she danced specially for Queen Elizabeth when the two monarchs met in a fairytale setting in Nuku'alofa.

These men formed the nucleus of our crew. But it is in the Tongan tradition of life that a man, seeing friends working, and having time on his hands, will go and join them for a while. If, for instance, we had been building a house, every passer-by would have sat with us awhile and plaited some of the leaves. This was a job that anyone could do. But rebuilding the vessel was a specialist's job; only a few of our friends could lend a casual hand. Some of them came often and became permanently associated with us; some drifted in for a brief visit and after they went away we did not see them again.

4

It was a joy to work in the peaceful sunshine of the sea verge. *Velata* lay alongside the coastal road where it was entered by occasional traffic from the small-boat wharf incomprehensibly named the Yellow Pier; and from the sleepy streams of movement friends and admirers were often diverted our way.

There probably isn't a seaman in the world who doesn't revel in the smells of fresh wood-shavings in all their great variety, of tar and rageen and red-lead-and-oil, of brine-drenched wood and old hemp and new cotton. There is nothing in the world more pleasant than working at your ease beside the sea, on sand-rimmed turf, under a moderate sun. When, as in Nuku'alofa, the eye is also charmed by the columns of coconuts with their vast bouquets of leaves, by the pastel flowers of bauhinnias and the strident masses of colour in the African tulip-trees, by the dozen islands floating in the bay, the patient sails, the wind-flecked water, and the happy laughing faces of children who have never known the sorrows of frustration or the dismal rewards of dissatisfaction and self-pity, then even work that could be dreary becomes a routine of joy.

There was an ebb and flow in our numbers comparable to the ebb and flow of the harbour waters, and sometimes occasioned by it; for at low water a congress of food-seekers wandered out to the edge of the reef, and sometimes a man or two of ours would be among them. Most of these fishers, though, were women or girls. Dressed as for the street, and carrying an iron rod with which to break the coral, they combed every inch of the bay, venturing far out, and sometimes going completely underwater to lay hold of some titbit, an octopus or a large shell, in the depths of a pool or a channel. Sometimes one would struggle with an octopus for a quarter-hour or twenty minutes. She might have an audience, a group of men who wanted the devil-fish for bait in deep-sea fishing, perhaps; and then it would be sold as soon as it was captured.

Ve'etutu watched while a woman struggled in a foot of water with an antagonist we could not see.

"She's having too hard a job," I said after nearly half an hour; and as I spoke the woman threw herself down on her belly in the water and her yellow dress darkened to brown and clung to her skin as she probed the depths of a crevice in the reef.

"But she will get it," Ve'etutu said confidently. "She will not give up, because she is a sister of my wife and she comes from Ha'apai."

And indeed, after a few more minutes the woman captured the octopus.

Down on the Yellow Pier someone called to Ve'etutu.

"He wants to buy the octopus," Ve'etutu explained to me.

"See if he will pay me a shilling," the woman asked, giving up the fish. She was laughing and happy, shy in my presence, but apparently not at all conscious of the appearance of her dress, wet and mud-streaked, that a

41

few minutes before had looked so pretty; nor of the cold wind that plastered it to her skin.

"She wants two shillings," Ve'etutu told the buyer, and he paid without hesitation. His sister-in-law beamed with happiness when she caught the coins. The tide was coming in, putting an end to the hunt, but she had another octopus, in a burlap bag, for the family meal.

About ten of us worked on *Velata*, and it seemed that there was never more than one tool for each man. We had a ripsaw, a crosscut, a hammer, a woodrasp, an adze, a breast-drill, a brace with two bits only, a plane, a chisel, and an axe. If there were any tasks beyond the capacity of this collection a tool was made for the purpose. Drill-bits, for example, were hammered out of any handy scrap of metal.

Waste was kept to an absolute minimum. Offcuts of wood were saved to provide small fittings; the final chips used to feed the fire were less than palm-sized. We cut six large sweeps from solid baulks of timber ten inches wide. Above the blades the offcuts were carefully sawn into half-inch planks, and provided all the gratings that protected every part of *Velata's* interior not decked.

In a finishing operation I started punching the heads of the nails that secured the gunwale capping, but David stopped me.

"It makes a good job, Olefi. But then I have to use putty to fill the holes up, and I can't afford putty. Drive the heads flush and leave them. They'll rust, but they'll last the season."

It was the same with every finished job in Tonga. Americans particularly were quick to criticize and comment on inadequacies they saw. But these inadequacies arose not from laziness or ignorance but from the impossibility of buying supplies. They were caused by poverty, for which Tongans have always learned to find a compensation. Not a pound of putty was bought for *Velata*. The small amount we used was contrived by finding old hardened chunks of putty about the site, where people had worked vessels for a century, by pounding these to a powder, and by working the powder again to the appropriate consistency after adding fresh oil from coconuts and candlenuts and the rest.

Every used nail in every piece of timber was rescued, straightened, and given fresh purpose. No money was spent without careful thought. When the time came to replace the rudder of the launch *Kaimoana*, David took a plan of the main metal part to the Government Stores, where boiler-plate was sold and where the charge was made according to the weight of metal used. The amount of work saved in this way was considerable, because Government machines did the cutting to shape and there was no excess metal to pay for.

David returned empty-handed, and it was easy to see he had lost his normal composure. The well-tried system of the Government Stores was to weigh the piece remaining rather than the piece cut off and to estimate the chargeable balance from the last book entry. This they regarded as a reasonable precaution that wastage under the flame would be paid for. But when David was asked to pay for sixty and more pounds of metal instead of the twenty-five under his arm he objected. Someone had stolen a section of the boiler-plate, but the Government Stores were determined not to take the loss. They had the previous recorded weight, and the loser would be the next man to buy metal. David declined the honour. He left the embryo rudder and walked out.

"Fair enough," I commented. "But we'll still have to buy the metal somewhere—and there isn't anywhere else."

"Not so bad as you think," returned David. "Nobody's going to want that shape of a rudder in boiler-plate, because there isn't anyone else in Tonga just now slipping a boat with an iron rudder. So we'll be able to buy the piece at scrap prices instead of plate prices. Wait a week or so and see."

He proved ninety per cent right. In the week we waited someone bought six small disks of plate in that weight—and the Government Stores unfeelingly cut them out of our rudder. So, when David returned for it, it had assumed a most unconventional shape. But it was cheaper than ever, and since its underwater appearance did not greatly matter, we made use of it. It had retained sufficient balance. We had to fasten it to the bronze shaft with copper rivets once more, though we knew that electrolytic action would immediately begin to rot the metal away again when we launched the boat into sea-water. But the devil was driving and our needs were served.

Since we bought nails a pound at a time, timber as it was needed, and paint when its absence could no longer be ignored, and since everyone contributed according to his capacity, it was difficult to estimate our expenses; but they totalled something like £500 for the two boats and all the gear. No wages were paid and none were asked. Food was available to the workers most of the time: some of them took turns in providing it from their gardens or from those of their relatives and friends. Friends are survival insurance in these happy islands, and everyone has a surplus of cover. But if one man went without, the probability was that all did; even the children at times would be sent off to a day at school without anything to eat. They went uncomplainingly and took direct measures to lighten their load: they climbed up fanpalms for the nuts, or ate green mangoes hardly come to size, or gnawed on anything available.

A Polynesian genius for improvisation, which rises

to Everest heights in Tonga, was called upon for almost every operation. It was necessary to stretch the whale-line and take the kinks out of it. Since it was a 4½ inch sisal rope 120 fathoms long this looked like becoming a tiresome operation. And so it would have been, by any method familiar to me. But in Tonga it was no trouble, no trouble at all. The heavy line was carefully tied about three coconut palms in such a way as to offer temptation to school-children. Every day when they came racing from their classrooms, convoys of from thirty to forty at a time made for the rope, and swung and bounced on it, and performed prodigies of athletic prowess; and when darkness had called them away. Ve'etutu would take in the slack. Two weeks of this painless manipulation and the sisal was fit for use.

In an operation of prime importance the loggerhead was completely removed from the little ship and rein-stalled. The loggerhead is the post or bollard round which the whale-line runs and by which the boat is towed when the whale is hit, since two or three turns of the line are taken round it at the beginning of the con-test. It is the focal-point of the whole strain applied by the whale. It is situated always in the stern of the boat and increases the hazards, for the running line thus tra-verses the whole boat and endangers every man in it. This often puzzles the armchair whaler, since if the bollard and the line-tub were positioned forward, no one but the harpooner would be in any danger from the writhing racing rope. But the reason for it is simply that the line must be available to every hand. Every muscle in the boat is needed to play the whale, and with the loggerhead astern the men have the full length of the whaler in which to lay to and get a purchase. They can all pull without getting in one another's way.

The danger is extreme, but is in some degree coun-tered by precautions. A bush-knife or an axe is always kept by the loggerhead to part the line; a small hand-axe is also socketed, less dangerously, by the fairlead in the bow—these being the two points at which the rope under strain makes contact with the material of the boat, and therefore the two points at which a cut may expeditiously be made. Thus either headsman or boat-steerer (who are normally, on a small expedition, the whaling-master and the sailing-master) can make the decision to sacrifice expensive gear and lose the quarry. The death or loss overboard of either man does not upset this safety arrangement.

The hand-axe in the bow has a double function. It is used as a hammer by the headsman, who must straighten out his irons after each use. This is another essential, for the metal used in the shafts of harpoons and lances must be of the softest types compatible with strength.

On *Velata* we rebuilt the whole area round the loggerhead and added a deck, six inches below the gunwale, for the helmsman and the sheet-hand. On this deck, too, the coiled part of the mainsheet was kept away from any relationship with the whale-line. The latter was kept in a tub on the main deck at the bottom of the boat and abaft the centre-board box; and surrounding this tub—more precisely, a cut-down oildrum —we would carry eight or ten hundredweight of sand ballast in sacks.

Except for the newly installed gratings, the areas abreast of the centre-board box were left alone, to become small storage areas for fish caught, for fenders, and for other items not easily damaged by sea-water, because the wash of the bilge slopped back and forth.

Since I'd built boats before, since for years I'd made repairs to my own small craft and, being short of money, had learned a great many improvisations and short cuts on my own account; since throughout a lifetime I'd learned to make the best use of unconsidered trifles, my workmates in remarkably short time accept-

46

ed me almost as one of themselves. At first they tended to be over-solicitous if, say, I cut myself; but our relationship quickly adjusted to less artificial levels.

Each lunchtime I excused myself from their company and wandered home for a meal. The Tongans didn't interrupt their working-day to eat. One meal a day, or at the most two, was sufficient for them. They ate breakfast if leftover food happened to be in the house, and then they ate it without any ceremony, just to stay their hunger, and probably while they were on their way to the day's destination. Any time they were hungry there was always a coconut of which to eat the white meat or drink the liquid; or perhaps they would find a cooked sweet potato, or a root of tapioca, or even a piece of the yams they loved best of all.

Their attitude to food was hardly understandable to people with European backgrounds. Food connected with a feast is of prime importance to a Tongan; it has to be of good material, it has to be cooked by the men and mainly in earth ovens, it has to be prepared to an exact perfection. But of major importance is that it should come whole to the table. No quantity of sliced ham can show the respect to guests that Tongans feel is accorded by the presentation of a small but whole pig cooked on a spit. At feasts crabs and crayfish are also presented whole; the compliment to the guest envisages that he may take any part of the whole animal. No guest could cope with more than a small fraction of the food laid out for him. When Queen Salote entertained Queen Elizabeth, six hundred pigs were on the tables, entire and delicious.

I often heard tourists and temporary residents discuss the great wastage such prodigality involved, but in my opinion these judgments were wholly superficial. I have never seen any evidence of waste. When the primary guests finish with the feast and leave the heaped mountains of delicacies, the secondary guests move in and finish any considerable portions remaining. At the end of their session, in all probability, a tertiary sitting will gnaw the bones left by their predecessors. The dogs, which circle the site so distantly that it is obvious they have been trained on a hundred other occasions, might get to lick the leaves upon which the feast has been spread; they are unlikely to have more substantial luck.

In such dispositions everyone knows his place. There is no jostling for advantage. The serving people are last to eat. There is no servant class in Tonga, though in the old days there were slaves and these were a separate caste. In the Tonga of today everyone serves in his turn and counts it a privilege. There is no compulsion on him; if he does not feel like work there is no reason for him to do it. The chances are, however, that he will, and that his temporary servitude will leave him with a glow of pride.

Outside the social structure of the feast, food means very little to the Tongan and a fast of a couple of days is not considered a hardship. Such a fast would be undertaken if food were not at hand, or if a person felt he needed the discipline. The getting of meals is not allowed to interfere with other pursuits.

My absences to eat the midday meal to which a sometimes civilized life had accustomed me gave me an opportunity of watching the workaday Tonga, and in a short while, from a vantage of familiarity. As often as not I walked past the unpretentious building where, at that period, Parliament was nearly always sitting.

Opposite, there was a great spreading fig-tree on the *mala'e* and beneath it the Cadillacs of Deputy Premier Tu'ipelehake and one or two of the other noblemen would stand, almost alongside the notices that forbade the green to vehicles. It was a democratic rather than an aristocratic transgression; the Cadillacs followed the lead of less sumptuous vehicles, the advantage being that the drivers could enjoy the shade. They stood alongside the cars, alert to catch the first sign of an employer emerging from the House, which looked like nothing more than a small Wesleyan chapel. The Parliamentarians used a tiny door in the side of the building, a door that looked too small for the passage of Prince Tu'ipelehake or his larger elder brother, the Premier, Prince Tungi, whose weight was reputed to be close to four hundred pounds.

Sometimes there were ordinary citizens of Tonga waiting a chance to talk to the nobles who made up the majority of Parliamentarians; and when these or any one of them appeared I would note a curious little happening. The men seeking the audience would sink to the ground with their legs folded, in the yogi's lotus position or something like it, and they would clasp their two hands into a single fist. In this position they would conduct their conversation with the noble, who would remain standing.

It was one of the distinguishing marks of caste, and undoubtedly it derived from more robust times when the rulers had ample reason to fear men of the lower ranks. The position was the same as that ordained for the kava ceremony; from it no threatening act could be followed through; the man sitting, locked by his own muscles into an attitude from which recovery would be slow, was completely at the mercy of the man standing.

Today the Tongan still invests the action with importance and gives it the deliberation it deserves. He does not adopt it in a comfortable conformity with tradition. When he passes the house or the vehicle of royalty or the higher nobility he salutes and experiences an inner glow of pleasure at the performance of this duty. He never feels debased in such actions, as people with less confidence do. People of other nations may believe, if they care to, in the unwieldy triad, Liberty, Equality, and Fraternity; the Tongan, who perceives very clearly that any one of these antagonizes at least one of the others, doesn't waste time or consideration upon any such concept. He knows that men are not equal, and settles happily for the combination of Liberty and Fraternity which has distinguished the Polynesians in their islands as far back into history as man can probe. Of these he makes certain, as no republican anywhere can be certain as long as he clings to the delightful fantasy of Equality. For even between man and slave there was a friendly relationship in the Tongan past, and the highest of mortals was and is attended by his *matapule,* a commoner born who can take surprising liberties with his person and his property.

The great fig-tree seemed not to have changed a fraction since its likeness had been used, nearly forty years before, to distinguish the common Tongan penny stamp. Elsewhere the *mala'e* was shaded by majestic casuarinas, trees with a dignity much appreciated by the Tongans, who plant them at cemeteries and places like the Mala'e Pangai, where important guests are feted, or the Mala'e Kula, the Red Field, where Tonga's royalty lies buried.

The wind still sings in the needles of these casuarinas, but the song is not as insistent as it is where the trees most like to grow. Their preference is for the long sand-spits that throughout the South Pacific on the right locations reach directly into the south-east trades, pointing like weather-vanes to the source. On the *mala'e* you have to listen closely for the sweet sighing sibilance for your attention is enwebbed by the louder sounds of human song and laughter, and of friend calling to friend.

At the front of the *mala'e* opposite the wharf, is the Post Office, and here, twice a week or so, I made a call for mail. To be sure, the aircraft came only once, and one call should have been sufficient; but I had so many friends at the Post Office and my friends were so solicitous that when they saw mail addressed to me they put it aside, so that they could lay hands on it at once when I appeared, passing it out over the heads of customers earlier on the scene. Sad to say, as often as not my friends were not there when I arrived, and the letters were not in the proper place. But a day or two later they would see me passing, or on an impulse I would decide to call, or they would send a lad to the house with the letters, or run down to *Velata* with them; and there I'd be, with the delightful gift of letters in mid-week, when I least expected them. The delay didn't usually make any difference. As there was a week be-tween mails there was no point in having all my letters too soon.

Tall hoop pines, twice and three times the height of the mature coconuts, border the *mala'e* on the sea side, where the road runs from the eastern end of the town to the Post Office, and then strikes inland, to become Taufa'ahau Road, the main shopping street. Where the road turns, the pines march straight on, past the tidy green lawns that on steamer days are hidden under the beautiful artifacts sewn and woven and carved and laid out for sale, and right up to the stone wall surrounding the red and white Royal Palace, built a century ago of New Zealand kauri pine, and in pristine condition yet.

The palace wall borders the western side of the *mala'e,* and on the southern side, small, individual, and altogether charming, are the administration offices. The first is a cottage with comfortable verandas and perpetually open doors. It is shared between Maile-tonga, the palace secretary, and Ve'ehala, who, under the Queen, heads the Traditions Committee and per-forms other functions affecting Tongan arts and the study of history.

Next door is the dental clinic, beset with lawn-lounging clients, the satisfied customers with their heads bandaged pudding-cloth fashion, as I haven't seen dental patients for years; and I can't help thinking there is probably some comfort in the style. The administration offices, at the foot of Taufa'ahau Road, look vaguely Swiss, an impression heightened by the Tongan flag waving above the spire, a red flag with a red Geneva cross in a white canton.

Taufa'ahau Road, where the shops were, was a lively exciting thoroughfare, particularly on Saturday mornings. Then the villagers came in from remote parts of the main island and, in crowded luggers, hundreds on a vessel licensed for twenty or so, from other islands in all three groups. From early morning, cross-legged on bright clean mats, they lined the streets to sell vast quantities of produce.

Only thirty years before, the first carts rumbling into Nuku'alofa with produce to sell were stopped by the horrified residents of Veitongo, perhaps the most conservative of the main island's settlements. The Veitongo villagers were shocked beyond measure that anyone should even think of selling food. Food was provided by nature, and it seemed against the dispositions of God that it should not be as free as flowers.

But the urbanization of the Tongan was inevitable. Nowadays everything edible comes to the market and some produce, eggs for example, is dearer in Nuku'alofa than in New York, London, or Sydney. It is even conceivable that some day someone is going to ask a price for flowers, though if prayers are answered, that day is still a long way off.

There are few stalls. The typical vendor sets out her wares on the mat in front of her—taro roots by the dozen; long tubers of fresh tapioca; the green leaves of taro for making *lu,* which tastes like spinach and is a delicacy when baked in coconut cream; heavy stalks of bananas in several varieties, but always green; oranges, green in colour but sweet to the taste; breadfruit in season and mangoes and every other fruit; plaited

52

green baskets of sweet potatoes; and here and there a group of five perhaps, or seven eggs, nested in a cabbage leaf.

The sellers of oil group together; you can sniff at bottle after bottle of delicately scented oils while you make up your mind. The base is always a blend of coconut, candlenut and *feta'u,* the round nut of the Calophyllum that grows by most tropical shores; yet the choice is extensive. The oil comes in shades of green and amber and combinations between, the scents seem to be filched from every plant in the island—the root of a swamp reed, the bark of cinnamon, the flowers and fruits of a dozen varieties of trees and bushes. If you make a good choice your friends and the vendors will be forthright in their approval. If you don't, most will be equally loud in condemnation, though the maker—maybe your best friend—sits and listens, beaming through the criticism until she finds the opportunity for riposte.

To the eye, the Tongan crowd is not a gay one, not nearly as gay as the crowds in other island groups. Mourning for lost relatives is worn for months, and every Tongan is rich in relatives. Black, therefore, seems the favourite colour. For mourning or other occasions of moment the Tongan shows his best respect when, around his waist, he wears his oldest mats, tattered and faded and breaking away. Not infrequently these are put on over other clothes as tattered; poverty, material but never mental, shrieks its presence.

Bare feet are silent on the road. Voices furnish the undercurrent of noise; and enterprising auctioneers of secondhand clothes have added the horror of loudspeakers that dominate the market sounds.

When it was not market day I loved to wander home by the back streets, where life flowed in a pleasant serenity. The wide lawns were not only cut, they were swept each day, and the chirring of the besoms was a cheerful and inevitable morning sound.

Dotted everywhere among the cottages were trees, predominantly the breadfruit hung with generous green moons that were rinded with a heavy criss-cross graining—the bread-tree

> . . . which, without the plough-share yields
> The unreaped harvest of unfurrowed fields
> And bakes its unadulterated loaves
> Without a furnace in unpurchased groves,

as Byron noted, a little enviously, I have always thought.

The breadfruit in its seven or eight varieties adorns every yard; only the mango, a little less numerous, is a more impressive fruit-tree. The fruit called *vi*, which Cook and Wallis translated as "apple" seems to grow everywhere too, and is much esteemed in its short season. Its leaves, which also resemble those of a well-nourished apple-tree, are usually pierced to lacework by the jaws of some infesting insect.

The bark of the candlenut provides a brown dye essential to the age-old art of printing patterns on tapa cloth. So much of the bark of suburban trees is pared away each year that the continued survival of the tortured specimens is miraculous. The nuts contribute their oil to the delicate Tongan cosmetic; they also provide a purgative that is violently effective.

The commanding columns of the African tulip-tree flare like paint-splashed cumuli dark against the sky blue, the hibiscus and the croton blaze gaily from the variegated hedges, coconuts maimed of half their leaves sway in the upper levels of air, the small gardens are bordered with the dainty green and white of Eucharist lilies, and everywhere the children play near the flowers.

On my way I pass the bus stop where, as always, people are waiting. They are still there, a little more numerous, when I come back. Maybe a bus will come soon, maybe not, for the operators trundle out their vehicles only when a prickling of thumbs advises that the prospects of a load are promising. But no one looks strained or worried; no one wears a frown.

Back at the *Velata* the work is advanced by exactly as much as though I had been on the job the whole time. Our men work long hours, and happily, but except in emergency they never allow me to make a similar contribution.

5

I had business in the Government offices, and came down late to the beach. David's face was shining.

"It's possible we can get Totau to come and fish whale with us," he announced.

Completing the crew was a problem. There were not enough Minerva Reef survivors to carry the expedition and not enough of them knew the whaling game well enough. New additions to our company ought to be experienced men, but even in Tonga experienced whalers are hard to come by today. There are plenty of enthusiastic volunteers, but their potential must be measured against their background and their experience. They must be chosen with care, for enthusiasm is not enough.

Totau would be an acquisition indeed. At the age of forty he had already become a legend in Polynesian whaling circles for a single exploit that bordered upon the realm of utter fantasy and has possibly never been equalled in the history of the world. He caught a whale and killed it without assistance; and, at least in the closing stages of the affair, he did it without a boat. He also did it without explosives; others have accounted for whales single-handed, but not with the equipment to which Totau was limited.

I've never heard of a similar exploit, nor seen any mention of one in the whaling books I've read, though some of them relate stories that seem to verge on legend. There is no doubt about the authenticity of Totau's adventure as there is no exaggeration in its details; the affair is attested by too many independent spectators, not all of them shipmates of his.

Some of those who had been his shipmates on that occasion were already in our company. The incident had its beginnings with Maile's boat, the *Vaisingano,* the whaler stolen by the three lads who set out for America and abandoned by the Japanese fishing captain in a storm. Maile Siakumi was captain, and Ve'etutu Pahulu his sailing-master. Maile's brother Fa'aui was the headsman, and two others in the crew were Saimone and this Totau Samisoloa. They were fishing whale out of Ha'apai, which meant that they could operate within a few miles of their homes. It also meant that, if they were successful, the sale of meat would be a problem; there was appetite but not much money in the islands of the home group and they could not tow a kill far enough to reach a better market.

It was a perfect day about the middle of the dry monsoon of 1958, a day of bright sunshine, with a calm sea and a light breeze, sufficient to give them excellent sailing without dampening a humpback's desire to bask. They sighted a large cow with a medium-sized calf.

The bay whalers have a never-ending discussion as to the best tactics to follow in this event. Some prefer to harpoon the mother first, making sure of the larger, more important return, and then, at a later opportunity, to lay rope on the calf. It will still be around, in all probability, even if the death struggles of its mother are unduly protracted. The mother will fight the less because of her worries about the calf; her attention will be divided to the end.

The other school believes that the calf should be taken first. It can be the more quickly dispatched, and the mother will no more abandon the dead body than she would the living youngster. After the calf has been killed the mother will make an easy victim.

Both theories are based on generalizations that individual whales have disproved. In practice, too, the situation dictates the technique. When the whaler is committed to her final approach the headsman harpoons the nearer victim; if the two whales are equally available, which is most unlikely, he will follow his own judgment, which may be swayed by any one of a number of factors.

On this day they ran up quite readily upon the unsuspecting pair, and Fa'aui harpooned the cow. She was a big animal, around the fifty-foot mark, which in a humpback is massive and probably indicates a weight of more than sixty tons. The calf was a young one, only two or three months old, and probably about a third of the cow's weight. When the harpoon struck, Maile lowered the sails and Ve'etutu, on the tiller, held *Vaisingano* in line with the towrope, as closely as he could. Fa'aui, Maile, Saimone, and the remainder of the crew except Totau hauled down on the whale-line and, very shortly after the first flurry, closed the gap between boat and whale.

Totau had taken the lance to deliver the final thrust to the cow, and the others, by hard unremitting efforts on the line, saw to it that he had excellent opportunities. He had difficulty finding what the old-time whalers used to call "the life"; he stabbed and stabbed with the lance, giving fifty or sixty deep thrusts before he much diminished the power of the cow to struggle.

In all this time the calf never left her mother. Unhampered by any line and unwounded, frightened moreover by the intrusion of disaster upon the idyll of the tropic day she wheeled ahead and away again and again, leaving her mother behind at almost every stroke of her wide fins, but each time returned, suppressing her panic, to seek safety, or more probably solace, in the familiar black proximity of her dam.

When death or its close approach stopped the course of the cow the calf became frantic, returning to butt against the great inert body, a body that by this time was occupying the whole attention of the crew. Of all the crew, that is, save Totau.

Totau seized a spare harpoon which carried about twelve fathoms of line, ready for bending on to the main whale-line, and thrust it deep into the calf. There was an immediate chorus of protests from his companions. They had their hands full with the dead cow. Her mouth had to be sewn up—if it were left open she would, on being towed, fill with water and sink. A hole had to be bored through the short protuberance of her dorsal fin for the attachment of a line to ensure safe towage. The whale-line had to be unbent from the harpoon that was sunk in the flesh, and lashed to another to be sunk at the best place on the body for efficient towing bitts. All this had to be done in an ocean with a quota of sharks whose interest had been aroused by the gallons of blood that had been pouring into the water since the first strike. A whale has proportionately much more blood than any other animal; blood is oxygen-storage, and the protracted immersions accompanied by violent underwater exertion necessitate huge quantities. During the long contest this severely injured whale had spread her blood widely in the sea.

The crew members were not happy with their lance-man for harpooning the calf at this stage. It might have been possible to handle it; indeed it is well established that whale-boats have made two or more kills simultaneously, incredible though it sounds; but there was no point in this kind of action here, for the calf would have stayed near by. Now it was certain to become a greater nuisance still, and they risked losing the mother.

Their complaints were loud and to the point. Maile, normally the most phlegmatic of men, a supremely self-confident fellow, able to cope with most emergencies in silence, was loudest of all.

"You're mad," he said. You're silly in the head. You're crazy. You've lost even the few brains you were born with."

To make matters worse, Totau lost the harpoon. With her wound the calf might well decide to abandon her mother. The complaints grew more pointed.

"I'm sorry, boys," Totau said. "I know I did the wrong thing. But don't worry. Go ahead with what you're doing, because I'm going to square this."

He took still another harpoon, cut twelve fathoms from the other end of the whale-line—the section that had not been drawn from the line-tub by the first run of the cow—and bent it to the harpoon. Then as the calf came in again he harpooned her once more, raising still more wails from his companions.

"Stay where you are, boys, because I have this matter under control. I'll handle it myself. I've made trouble for you, I know, and now I'm going to set it right," he said, and dived over the side into the red water.

To a European it seems at least unlikely that a man in this situation would make such a speech. To a Polynesian, that was the spice of the moment. The speech was probably made in the most restrained and decorous of tones, the voice nicely modulated, the words carefully chosen; for in the moment of departure Totau would have been well aware that he was in conception with a legend. He knew that the stories would survive whether or not he proved successful in his mad enterprise.

He had thrust the harpoon home deep, and now he was in the sea, being towed by the baby whale. Possibly he expected that she would remain close to her mother, that all he had to do was to act as a living marker-float until his companions had finished with the cow. But the second harpoon was too much for the baby; in pain or panic she headed for the horizon, towards the small inhabited island of Mango, a lesser unit in the Ha'apai group, not much more than a dry reef lifted just above the level of the sea.

From time to time, but not as often as an adult would have done, she dived; and when she did, Totau clung tightly to the rope. He had excellent lungs and long training in controlling them underwater. He was fortunate too in the baby's excess of panic; she did not dive deeply or stay under for long but haunted the surface, blowing at short intervals of three to four minutes.

For the shallower parts of the dive Totau so manipulated the rope that he could stay on the surface, sometimes remaining there until the whale came up again. When she was on the surface and momentarily still, he worked his way along the line until he reached her side. There, as best he could, he jabbed the harpoon deeper. The primary effect of this was simply to spur the little whale to new efforts, and Totau was taking dangerous liberties with the great sweep of the fins, formidable weapons half as long again as himself. As the whale leapt away Totau took new holds in the heavy whale-line, paying it out; the wet rope ripping at his skin, hard as a wood-rasp.

Quite early in the ride came the incident that to me is the most amazing of the whole crazy affair. The whale made one sustained dive and at a certain depth Totau knew himself unable to follow down any more.

He released the rope entirely, surfaced, and swam hard in the direction he believed the whale to be travelling. His judgment or his luck was good; she surfaced and stopped close enough for him to swim and recover the loose rope. He worked his way up to the harpoon again.

The wooden handle had not released after its first impact, as in its design it should have done, but was in position; and again he thrust the iron into what he hoped were the vital parts of the whale. She dived deep once more, and this time Totau stayed with an unbroken hold throughout the dive. When she came to the top her death was near.

All of this had happened in the channel that separates the islands of Nomuka and Mango, and some of the men from tiny Mango, having observed the primary capture of the cow whale manned a cutter and came out to offer what assistance they could.

"Don't worry about us," Maile shouted when they came near the *Vaisingano*. "We're all right. But if you follow the little whale you'll find a man in tow of it."

As he spoke the little whale was already more than a mile away, and by no means near the end of its travelling.

By the time the Mango cutter caught up with it, Totau had delivered the finishing stroke, the whale was on the surface dead, and the sharks had gathered. Totau greeted the men a little breathlessly, but still politely, still with a considered choice of words, and established his personal claim to the whale. He was delighted to accept their help.

Most of the men in either party were too excited by the whole event to estimate the distance the whale had swum with Totau playing drogue in her wake. Some of them believed it to be five miles; one or two said it was not so much. There was no difference of opinion about the size of the baby, however. When it was measured on the beach it ran to a trifle shorter than thirty-two feet in length; it was therefore something much more than twenty tons of lively tug for Totau to cope with.

The Tongan is always quick to make the appropriate gesture on all deserving occasions, and when the Mango cutter returned with Totau and his catch to the *Vaisingano*'s side, Totau, with the full support of Maile, Ve'etutu, and Fa'aui, offered the calf as a gift to the island of Mango. The islanders were poor people, and probably could not have raised much money anyway; but that was far from the point. A good story deserves a good ending, and the Mango people feasted till the whale, kept briefly in the cool sea, was reduced to the dimensions of the seed of a legend. The cow was towed to Nomuka, and she brought the whalers an adequate return.

The legend has not grown, nor will it till the whalers who manned *Vaisingano* are dead or waiting for death in the scented sunshine. And after that its growth will be inhibited by the delineating influence of print. But what would have happened to such a story in the days before the means of accurate record? In Polynesia there are many stories of friendships between man and whale, and it seems to me possible that they may have been triggered by some such incident.

In Tonga there is no tradition of man actually hunting the whale in pre-European times; but I thought it important to know exactly how these isolated Polynesian mariners regarded the great whales that shared their familiar seas, and I took the problem to Ve'ehala. His post on the Traditions Committee is an important one. Queen Salote is most concerned to preserve and promote the arts of her little country, and Ve'ehala spear-points the organization she has built for this purpose on an earlier foundation. The Traditions Committee must approve of songs written to be played publicly in Tonga—on Tonga Radio, for example. The kava ceremony must be carried out to its exact specifications; the best of dancers come under its critical scrutiny. The Queen herself is most active in this proper enterprise. Ve'ehala devotes his life to it. He is, therefore, the great authority on Tongan tradition and history; though frequently other nobles—and other chiefs and commoners for that matter—are as personally concerned.

To Ve'ehala, then, in his little breeze-cooled office close to the palace wall. He was to get to know me well, for I brought him a great many inquiries. No matter how busy he might be his smiling composure was never ruffled, and he never spoilt a tale because of time pressures. He checked his every story against copious notes written in a series of black-covered notebooks kept conveniently in a desk drawer. And though his solicitude may have been dictated by his natural courtesy as much as by his position, no detail was too insignificant for his attention.

He told me of Lo'au, a chief of ancient Tonga who went with his companions to look for the horizon, to find an end to it, or a beginning. Lo'au went on and on, through Odyssean adventures in which canoes were lost and men perished, until, of only two survivors, one called Kae went aground on an island in the night. On this he built a fire which he was tending when he felt a movement he thought to be an earthquake, and the land sank beneath him, and he was left floating on the wide sea once more.

Kae looked, and saw that what he had believed to be an island in a group was nothing more than one of eight large whales together, sleeping in the moonlight.

So he swam on, and with the dawn he came ashore upon a sandy beach, an empty beach, a bank above the surface of the empty sea. In the growth of the light he found it not quite empty. On the white sand a large white mound was raised and when the sun rose it offered him a shelter from the heat. He crawled under an overhanging part of the mound, exhausted from his swim, and went to sleep in the friendly shade.

At midday he started in fear, for a huge bird flew over and round, and came in for a landing, and alighted astraddle of the mound, which Kae now saw was its egg. The name of the bird was Kanivatu. It sat upon the egg, and Kae, since nothing worse could happen to him, lashed himself to the great scaled claw in its cloak of feathers.

In the afternoon the bird took off again, and flew far over the sea, in what direction Kae could not determine. But the bird flew fast, and there came a time when Kae saw an island below him. He loosed himself and fell down, and found himself in Samoa.

He walked the pleasant land until he came to the house of a chief named Sinilau, and Sinilau fed and sheltered him, and brought him back to an abundant health, for his trials and his fears had made him weak and ailing.

Among the great and potent attributes of this Sinilau was his friendship for a pair of great whales named Tununga and Tonga. When he had accustomed himself to the proposition that a man might own and command whales, Kae remembered his brief stay upon the whale that was one of eight, and he begged Sinilau to let him ride to his homeland of Tonga on the backs of these whales. Sinilau agreed.

Tununga and Tonga made short work of the passage and Kae had a pleasant voyage. At the end of it the whales cruised close to the reef, and told him to swim in and bring Tongan oil and a length of Tongan tapa cloth they could take back to Samoa to prove to Sinilau that they had accomplished their mission.

But Kae told them first to take him closer to the shore and, as he hoped, they went aground upon the sandy flats. Kae called to all the people then to come and kill the whales, and cut them up for the ovens; and the people came running. They killed Tununga, who was closest to the shore, but Tonga made a mighty effort and escaped with no more damage than a few spears stuck in his back. These were more than sufficient evidence of the truth of his story when he went back to Samoa to alert Sinilau to the treachery of Kae.

Sinilau asked all the Samoan gods to help him when he went to Tonga, there to take possession of the bones of his pet whale, and also the person of Kae, its betrayer.

They came to Tongatapu at midnight, found and bound Kae, gathered the bones and took them all to Samoa. By virtue of the magic Kae did not wake till he got there. When he did, he heard cocks crowing.

"This is strange," he said aloud. "I could swear that those voices are the voices of the cocks that Sinilau kept in Samoa."

"For a very good reason," the voice of Sinilau replied.

His people parcelled Kae in the sugarcane leaves which give the finest of flavours to baked meats, and put him in an oven and cooked him. But they set out the bones of Tununga, all in place. Not really all, for his teeth had been left behind at the site of a feast in the village of Mu'a, in Tongatapu. But the people laid out the bones in their exact order without the teeth, and covered them with leaves and potent medicines, and the bones covered themselves with meat and skin again, and after nine nights Tununga came to life, and thankfully put out to sea.

Tonga's progeny became the sperm whales, properly fitted with ivory teeth; Tununga's became the humpbacks, with sunken, dished-in heads, and no teeth at all.

In New Zealand I had been familiar with a related Maori story in which a whale was owned by Tinirau who lived on the sacred floating island of Motutapu. He carried off Hine-uri, the sister-in-law of the demigod Maui, and fathered on her a son called Tuhuruhuru. With Tuhuruhuru's baptism in mind, Tinirau sent for the famous priest Kae, who thus became acquainted with Tinirau's pet whale Tutunui. Kae persuaded Tinirau to lend him Tutunui for the voyage home, egged the whale to destruction in the shallows of his home coast, and was subjected to an avenging death when he was captured by the women of Tinirau's tribe in a masterpiece of subterfuge.

In another Maori story a priest was abandoned to his death on the waterless volcano in the Bay of Plenty in the North Island. This volcano is called Whakaari by the Maori people, White Island by English-speaking New Zealanders. A *tohunga* or priest was safe from actual violence, for his person was sacred, though he was feared. But since no violence was envisaged, no superstitious fears saved the priest from this abandonment when, on a birding expedition, he fell asleep in a cave there. He had no way of signalling to his friends on the mainland, for the island was covered with smoke. Instead he called to mighty Tangaroa, the god of the sea, and to Tutara-Kauika, the king of all the whales, a mighty sperm whale. Tutara-Kauika came attended by a whale almost as big as himself, and delivered the *tohunga* safely to the mainland.

The *tohunga,* whose name was Te Tahi o Te Rangi (The First of the Heavens), lived a long time more, building a new house distant from his betrayers but in full view of the island where they had marooned him—the better, perhaps, to remember his lesson. When he died his spirit entered the ocean and he became a sea-god, a *maraki-ahu.*

There is only the one story in the traditional Tongan repertoire. A nation which had much commerce with the whales would probably have had more legends, so it seems likely that the Tongans had no more than an accidental acquaintance with the leviathans until the first of the European whalers, the *Port-au-Prince,* made her disastrous contact with the Friendly Islands. From that day on Tongans were sought as crewmen for the whalers, their qualities were highly esteemed, and they were more than adequate to the demands of the task.

But there was no home-based industry in the islands until 1890. In the peak years of the sperm industry boats concentrated in the waters north of New Zealand, waters for which Tonga was a handy base, though a little distant, for the sperm liked open water. The shallows round the Tongan group were the domain of the humpback, a variety with a peculiar history of relationship to the deep-sea whalers. It was frequently the first whale hunted on a new ground, possibly because of its love for shallows, which gave it a habitat centred closely on convenient bases. Almost as frequently it was the first variety to abandon an exploited region, either from timidity or from intelligence. But the whaler had few regrets in leaving it for other quarry, for it was not a good mark at all.

In the tropics its season was a short one and did not coincide with the best months for the pursuit of the sperm. It carried less blubber than the right whale, and less, and shorter, baleen. It had huge flippers, each up to about fifteen feet in length, far greater than those of any other whale; and these not only made it more dangerous to approach but gave it an increased speed so that, before the machine age, it was more difficult to catch than the sperm or the right whale. There were many indications that its intelligence was superior to that of the sperm or the right whale, and it was a more formidable adversary for this reason too. And of course, like the other whalebone whales, it yielded no return from spermaceti or ambergris or whale ivory.

A few of the whale-ships anchored in the group's sheltered havens sent their pinnaces sailing after what quarry might cruise close to the islands, but this, while it provided an idyllic leisure, was a short-sighted policy from a financial viewpoint. In Tongan waters the prevalence of humpbacks seems almost to keep the sperm whales distant, and the sperms return the biggest profits.

This summer stamping-ground of the humpback is small; the area of maximum recorded capture does not spread as far west as Fiji nor as far east as the longitude of Samoa. It is a circle of about 400 miles' diameter centred almost squarely on the island of Eua, not far north of the Tropic of Capricorn.

The desirable sperm whale ranged regularly all year round from the Fiji group north and east to the Tokelaus and the Cooks, and from this broad limit southwest to Norfolk and Lord Howe islands, and farther again to within a comparatively short distance of the Australian coast, then north along its length to the Barrier Reef off Queensland, where some always seem to be coiling their slumbrous bulks in patterns completed by their friends, like kindles of large wet kittens.

The southern right whale, second in desirability to the sperm (at least in the South Pacific) did not cruise up into tropical waters at all; whalers who appreciated its abject lack of resistance sought it—in company with the sperm—on the Solander Ground, centred on New Zealand's Foveaux Straits and stretching east as far as the Chathams, and north to Cook Straits between the two islands. Or they would cruise the Vasquez Ground, centred on the lonely Kermadecs.

The whalers killed the southern right whale at the rate of 15,000 a year—considering the American total only, which recorded a slaughter of 193,000 in the peak between 1804 and 1817. The discovery of petroleum in 1859 saved the whale and shattered the weakening industry, but a remnant of whalers remained, and in the year 1888 a New Zealand-owned three-master based itself on the island of Nukupuli, nine miles from Lifuka in the Ha'apai group, and there remained two years, filling her holds with oil. In 1890 she sailed for her home port with her cargo completed.

She sailed without the youngest member of her crew, a lad of fourteen or fifteen whose first name seems to have been forgotten but who was surnamed Cook.

Young Cook was wholly committed to the idyll of the South Seas, and his experience must have been parallel to that which Melville outlines in *Typee*, except that Cook's was a coral island with none of the beautiful forest, the cooling streams, and the waterfalls that, with some feminine aid, ensnared the heart of Melville. In addition, Cook was surrounded by happy Christians, not at all savage.

At that tender age he had become enamoured of Liangiangi, a local girl living in the nearby island village of Holopeka. She was willing. He set up an establishment and allied himself with the life about him.

He must have been a handy lad, and during his vessel's long spell in sheltered waters he had applied himself well. After she sailed he specialized in the repair of boats and houses, making himself a desirable unit in the social structure of the village. He proved also to be an efficient blacksmith and wheelwright, trades that were becoming ever more valuable as the island rhythm accommodated itself to end-of-century innovation.

When there was nothing else to do he built himself a little boat, very much in the style of the whale-boats he knew, but smaller, neater, tighter-looking. It was about twenty-four or twenty-five feet long and less than a third of that in the beam, very simply rigged, with cleats instead of a horse for the sheet, and fuss reduced to a minimum.

At his forge he worked on harpoons, lances, and

70

whaling-spades. He picked up enough trained crewmen to go out after humpbacks. He scored immediate success, rendered down the oil, and saved it to sell to the itinerants who combined financial and hedonist reward by following the island schooner trade.

With no opposition Cook prospered, though at the prices he could command a large whale might bring him no more than £50. But transport and sale always gave him difficulty. To save transhipment and demurrage charges he determined, in 1912 when he was getting middle-aged, to shift his operations to a port used by overseas vessels. Nuku'alofa, with a large and growing trade in copra, had become such a port. Cook moved down to the tiny island of Tufaka, near the outer limits of the coral-bordered harbour of the capital, but close, too, to the well-used thoroughfares of the humpbacks. Here he could beach his whales and cut them up, here store the oil in his own premises, and from here readily ascertain and meet the schedules of overseas shipping so that he could cut out the middleman and his schooner.

He was attending more to the business side of whaling at this time because his son Ned, a lively, likely lad, was old enough to skipper the boats. In anticipation of a regular and well-regulated trade he built deep concrete vats, like tanks, on the island shore.

An unexpected development now changed the nature of his business, not rapidly, nor at once, but over a long period of years. The meat of the whale had always appealed to a few gourmands whose appreciation began to be respected, over the years, as more and more people tried the meat. In the small islands of the Ha'apai group this appreciation had no economic value, though some reward may have been made in valuable kind (for nobody had any money). In Nuku'alofa, the seat of Government and the administrative centre, there was a large and growing population that was meat-hungry. There were schools, mission headquarters, visiting ships, the police and army establishments, accumulations of people who mostly ate what they were given and could be fed from this cheap and nutritious supply. The fresh meat found a ready sale. The vast quantities in a single carcass ensured a wide distribution that added rapidly to the pool of potential buyers.

Sales of meat increased to a point at which they passed in value the sales of oil; a dry-skin whale might return nothing at all because of its lack of blubber, but there was always a sufficiency of meat, and this market was local and immediate in effect. Cook was handling his money the day he caught the whale. No part of the animal had to be kept long enough for the smell to become offensive, as it did during the long process of trying out blubber, and by and by the taste of the consumers was educated to the point at which the blubber became as acceptable as the meat. The poorest sections of the populace, scavenging among the unwanted bones, became ardent enthusiasts of whale consumption. And soon there was no need whatever to assign any part of the whale to the export trade.

The small boat that Cook first built proved so efficient that he made others on the original frames. As the older ones became uneconomic he sold them, but built others that were exact replicas: dainty, efficient, fast. He used a pair at a time, one to attack, the other to stand by.

In 1937 the Cook boys had taken over administration to the point where they introduced a harpoon gun, and in this season they took twenty-nine whales. Not even this vast quantity could sate the communal appetite, and bay whaling seemed firmly established as important in Tonga's economy. The headsman in that season was a New Zealand Maori. Firing at the thirtieth whale, the gun exploded, and his legs were crippled by the blast. It was the last Tongan attempt to use such machinery.

But the whalers still used explosives under certain circumstances. In a bad season—for example, in bad weather when the whales did not bask on the surface—the headsman lashed a fused plug of gelignite to his harpoon and lit the fuse before he launched it at the whale. If his cast was good and the harpoon struck deep, the whale ideally, would dive, and would have reached a shallow depth by the time the gelignite exploded. If the plug had been lashed at the correct distance from the blade, and if the harpoon had been sunk to the ideal depth in the victim's blubber and flesh, the explosion killed the whale, which then rose to the surface. If the gelignite exploded too close to the flesh of the whale because the harpoon was badly placed, too deeply sunk or too closely angled to the slope of the body at that point, if any of a dozen other mishaps perilled the headsman's intention, the explosive tore a hole in the flesh and body of the whale, which then sank beyond recovery.

The establishment of the exact degree of finesse necessary to kill and keep the whale when gelignite is used, the trial and rejection of new and additional methods and skills, the acquisition of a nicety of judgment, were achieved at heaven knows what cost in whale life; and even when it was perfected the method did not much appeal to the regular whalers. But most of them had enough respect for it to carry gelignite when they could, in case its use might be indicated by prevailing conditions or by an emergency.

And certainly gelignite made possible the entry of new men into the industry. Johnny Siola'a, one of the leading whalers in Tonga, first went fishing for the great beasts with a canoe which he operated single-handed. He would kill his whale, make fast to the carcass, then signal to summon help for the long and arduous tow.

By these direct means he secured two whales that brought him enough money to buy a whale-boat, and thereafter he took his rightful place in the aristocracy of the hunters. He must stand unique, certainly among those heroic seamen whose hunting methods have been recorded. In theory his methods seem reasonably easy to follow, but in practice few men have hearts so stout as to counterbalance the fragility of a Tongan canoe in contests with such giants.

Johnny Siola'a's place in the industry was necessarily below the established eminence of the Cooks. Their ancestor left his legacy in a dynamic approach to life that all the Cook family seem to share. They are almost the only people in Tonga who consistently hurry about their affairs; they have a determinedly energetic gait that singles them out at a distance, and an equally distinctive manner of using their hands.

These rival whalers kept a friendly distance. We of the *Velata* had no social commerce with them. We swapped no information, built up no conscious rivalries. But at all times we were brightly aware of their movements, and when the whalers were at sea in sight of the Yellow Pier our work slowed down a little while we took in every detail of their complement, their tactics, and their sailing efficiency. I would have watched anyway, for the whalers were beautiful in their element, and seemed to reflect the characters of their owners.

The boats of the Cook family were nervous as blood horses, light and lively; when they were white specks on the distant horizon their actions and reactions proclaimed their identities.

6

The rebuilding of *Velata* provided no outlet for the concentration of energy that packed Ve'etutu's chunky frame. Though when the mood took him he was one of the most energetic in the team and took a joy in demonstrating his abilities, his set duty was to guard our house, and from this he had small relief. His worst problem was boredom, but he was halfway to solving it when one day he appeared with a pack of playing-cards, complete or, more accurately, replete with elevens, twelves, red thirteens, and two jokers.

"Today we fight," he announced, and cleared a space at the table. He was a master at the three Tongan card games—Last Card, which was fast and tricky; Five Hundred, a highly developed form of gin rummy; and Sweepy, which, I'm afraid, still remains a complete mystery to me. That day saw the beginning of a keenly fought contest which completely wore the spots and corners from four packs of cards and provided us all with a comprehensive understanding of Tongan challenges and war-cries.

When Ve'etutu spoke in English it was with a notably slow and apparently thoughtful delivery. He spaced his words while he made his selection from a small vocabulary learned in an army unit and cluttered, therefore, with words of command and service usages. This inadequacy was painful to him, for he had the soul of a poet and, in Tongan, a notable reputation for his verse, which was much concerned with deep seas and a standing sail, or love and scented flowers.

He was so tough as to seem indestructible. He had proved it on Minerva Reef, but as if this were not enough, the proof was duplicated for me on a night when two louts, each much larger than Ve'etutu, made insulting remarks about Amelia, a girlfriend he was taking home. In two hits Ve'etutu stretched both louts on the ground; his hand was torn to the knuckle by the force of the blows, and some of his opponents' teeth were dislodged. But he delighted in the delicate components of a soft beauty.

His mind, which was fascinated by the beauty of words, was a storehouse of remembered incident and philosophical deduction. The circumlocutions and proverbial sayings of the Tongans were an everlasting joy, and his need for a precise communication was so pointed that sometimes, when he was talking to Madeleine or me, he would retreat into Tongan, apparently deeming it better that we should not understand than that he should not give exact expression to his thoughts when these concerned his imagery and his soul.

"My father," he said one day, "was a very big man, important, very rich, oh yes, very wealthy."

This was a surprise to me, for I had already heard a good deal about his father and his male ancestors for six generations back. We were walking the road to the hospital, to which I repaired daily at this time for the treatment of a coral sore on my leg, and my wife was with us.

"Not rich in money, you understand. But no, for that

76

is a small matter, to be rich in money. One can do without money, and he did, as I do, though sometimes his father had money, more money than my father had, so that he was able to go over the blue ocean to school in Aotealoa. New Zealand.

"But . . . we look to the front. He was like me. He was rich in women. You know how it is with me; I have a girl friend here and another there, and where will you find better girls? Wherever there's a pretty face there's a smile for Ve'etutu. You know that. You see that.

"Oh, I am very rich in good girls, nice girls. I have girlfriends everywhere, for I make the songs to sing to them, very beautiful songs. In Veitongo, that small place, I have eight girlfriends, the best girls in Veitongo. In Nuku'alofa I have thirty-one. Perhaps I have forgotten one or two. In Ha'apai too—oh, very much in Ha'apai. I grew up there. Ha'apai girls are best. There are none like them. My wife is a Ha'apai girl and she lives there now, and I love my wife better than anyone in the world, though I love Amelia from Veitongo very much; the next to best.

"And my father was the same. He was taller than me, a head taller—oh, very handsome. He had many girls; many, many girls; you could not count them. Wherever he went there were girls to smile at him and to lead him away, and he would not be cruel, so he would go with them. He loved them all, every one the same. He had many children too. He had a big family, and it is good to be one of a big family."

"How many brothers and sisters do you have, Ve'etutu?" I asked him.

"For myself: fourteen brothers but only three sisters."

"That was a big family," I agreed. "You all lived together in the same house?"

"Not all. With different mothers. Same father, you understand, but different mothers."

"How many brothers and sisters in your own house, then, 'Tutu?"

"In my own house, from my own mother, only one brother but four sisters."

"*Four* sisters?"

"Different fathers, you understand, Olefi."

We walked in silence for a minute or two while I digested this. Madeleine's face was a study.

"But outside the family, my father had more children."

"More still?"

"Oh, many more. That family, my family, that was just in Ha'apai, on our own island, where my father lived. But outside. . . ." He spread an expansive arm. "In Vava'u, in Tongatapu, over in Eua—why, in New Zealand he had three children, one a Maori and two Papalangi, two Europeans."

"What was he doing in New Zealand, 'Tutu?"

"Olefi, I told you. He went to school there. His father had the money and sent him to school."

It seems impossible to write a truthful description of the sexual morality of the Polynesian. It's tempting to skip the subject, absorbing as it is, for there is no consistency whatever in the island attitudes until you plunge to a great depth. The conclusion is inevitable that the licentiousness reported by so many writers is an inheritance of the whalers, the explorers, and the traders; yet even in the pre-European era the islanders in general had great sexual freedom in certain directions.

The modern writer who finds delight in recording female promiscuity in the islands probably judges the entire population by the conventional licence of the wharf-side trollops who, as you can read in a thousand books, will establish a relationship here with visiting yachts exactly as they will in Sydney or San Francisco, Greenwich Village or San Pedro or Sankt Pauli, exactly

as they will in any port. Some investigators and record-
ers may be flattered by the discovery that their motives
are not as commercial as they are elsewhere, but then
the Polynesian is not selfish or hungry. Another difference is that Polynesian girls do not lose caste for
their promiscuity alone, even with that other, much
larger section of the populace which utterly refrains
from conduct such as theirs.

This apparently uncritical acceptance of amoral behaviour is very widely misinterpreted. With the Fifita
girls and their associates we were to see young Polynesian females in a different light. The girls were naturally circumspect in their relations with males young and
old, but if their inclinations happened to lead them in
other directions they were surrounded by a set of conventions and customs that seemed sufficient to impose
chastity upon them. Their world under these conditions
afforded them few opportunities of meeting boys or
men other than in a crowded company, so that they
combined an apparent social ease with a remote unat-
tainability.

They were delighted to accompany us on walks
about the town, and it was some time before we realized that unless they did so, or unless they were running some short errand, they seldom left the vicinity of
the house. On dull days, when the Tongan loves to
swim, they would wait until we made the suggestion
and then, with great delight, accompany us to the harbour. They had to get permission for every such expedition, though some of them were nearly out of their
teens. If Madeleine and I were not there David might
take them, or an uncle, or some adult related to the
friends they accompanied.

If there was no one to take them they could not go
but had to remain near the house, busying themselves
with some of the light duties that fill the days of
Tongan women, or playing, or studying. In general they

needed no instruction to apply themselves to these delights and duties; and certainly they never had to be induced to play nursemaid to the thoroughly coddled youngsters with which the vicinity of every house abounded.

A boy could, of course, invite one of the girls, say to the pictures, but not alone. If her mother and her father were not included in the invitation the offer would be regarded with suspicion and rejected; indeed, the lad would be thought lacking in decency. To take his girl to the pictures might cost him the price of a dozen seats, for mother and father would not dream of going if it meant leaving the other girls unattended at home. But the presence of this company would not permit the boy to use his sweetheart's sisters as a shield while he whispered sweet fancies in her ear; mother and father would undoubtedly choose the positions most strategic for efficient supervision. If he planned to bring some friends as well, his invitation would certainly be rejected.

In spite of these restrictions some lads did take girls with their families to the local picture-show. And this testifies to the Tongan's selflessness.

A much less expensive process of getting acquainted with girls is to follow the old Tongan tradition of the kava ring. A boy will supply the kava root for a kava ring to which he will invite all his more trustworthy friends, and he will ask the girl of his choice to make kava for them. This is a good psychological move, implanting the idea that he has an interest in her. She sits with the kava bowl, her hands steeped in the drink, making and remaking fresh bowls for a matter of three of four hours usually, and sometimes until dawn; and in all this time the lovers do not exchange a private word unless it be in that language of love which employs eyes and elbows, expression and gesture. There is no stricture on talk, but it cannot be private. As like as not, mother and an aunt or two are bedded down near by, within sight and hearing of the ring.

Girls are practised in the fine art of making kava from the time they are very small; they know every detail of the ceremony and they are tireless in what seems like unrewarding work. But to non-Polynesian eyes the cause of romance seems little advanced by the custom.

Kochab, a visiting English yacht, brought Nako, a Cook Islander who had cruised a good part of the world, a fine lad with an engaging personality. When Ve'etutu persuaded his Amelia's father to join him in providing a feast and dancing for our entertainment, the crew members of *Kochab* were included in the invitation. And Nako, whose partnership of Amelia in the Tahitian *tamarei* was the hit of the evening, was obviously a little smitten by young Stella, with her bright-eyed, happy face. Stella was chaperoned by David, and all was well.

But there was consternation a few nights later when Nako came calling, paying his respects, as a Cook Islander or a Tahitian would not have done a few generations back and a Tongan does not do today. He wanted to take Stella to the movies, and her embarrassment was acute. She knew that she would be blamed for his interest, for leading him on and giving him the impression that she was available for such a radical departure from a young girl's programme, and she appealed to Madeleine before even seeing Nako. Not only was the proposed expedition out of the question, but it seemed to her highly undesirable that it should even be mentioned. Fortunately, Nako had announced his intention only to a couple of younger sisters when he arrived.

Madeleine provided an acceptable solution by inviting Nako to play cards in our house, a game in which Stella joined. Nevertheless, Stella's mother and some other elder relations joined the party, sat three or four feet away from the players, and made their presence gently felt until Nako, at the end of the evening, went home.

In spite of the assertions made by generations of writers, behaviour such as this is not a relic of the restrictions imposed by missionaries. Nor does it apply, and it never did apply, to the entire population, for there is and always was a section, found largely but by no means exclusively among the lower orders, where sexual promiscuity is accepted as normal. The great difference from our own system is that the Tongan, and the unspoiled Polynesian generally, does not know pretence.

For this reason a girl who has had sexual relations with boys does not attempt to hide the fact. She will discuss her experience as she discusses any other aspect of her life, neither more nor less avidly; and her friends and acquaintances will take it from there. Since, also, there are no lingual inhibitions in describing actions or attributes which in other tongues are not politely mentioned, conversation is sometimes surprisingly frank, and a stranger brought up to other conventions might be pardoned for believing that loose morals are a national characteristic. Nothing could be farther from the truth.

The circumstance that no blame attaches to the licentious may well bolster these false impressions; licentiousness is accepted as a characteristic, as for instance a crippled knee is a characteristic, or a beautiful singing voice.

Sue, a friend of the Fifita girls, was desperate for a job, for anything that would remove her from the humdrum of island life. When the publicity-loving skipper of an American yacht crewed otherwise by girls announced his intentions of filling vacancies from local aspirants, Sue was overjoyed and elected herself to the crew immediately. The skipper reserved judgment. He was not too enthusiastic, for he preferred to get hard work from his crew rather than guitar music, at the production of which Sue was adept; but he didn't have an opportunity of making up his own mind, for Sue was officially denied permission to leave the island for New Zealand.

"Prince Tungi didn't want Sue to go," Virginia said.

"Oh, why was that?"

"Sue likes making babies too much," explained Stella, flatly.

"She's all the time looking for boys and making babies with them," someone else amplified. "She was in Fiji a long time and she had no job there, and there was too much of this and Prince Tungi thought she would give Tonga a bad name."

"In that case, she very likely would."

"But there is nothing for me in Tonga," Sue said. "I am a good secretary. I learned to be a secretary, but there are twenty trained girls for every job. I apply for every job, but no. They do not want me. I think some day I will find a boy from a ship perhaps, and we will make love and when he goes away he will not forget me. Perhaps he will come back for me. Or he will send for me. And then I will leave Tonga where there is nothing for me to do.

"There was a boy from Brisbane. I took him home and I danced for him all the night, and I made sure that he would come again to Tonga, or at least he would write; but he wrote only one letter, and he does not answer me any more."

Sue's baby-making had been successful more than once, but babies are precious in Tonga and hers were brought up by relatives. Sue with her little ukulele, or with a borrowed guitar, was too self-possessed to be really a pathetic figure. She was brightly intelligent, speaking English much more beautifully than most English-speaking people, with a lilting, modulated accent that derived not from the level Tongan speech but from the remote island dialect of Niuatoputapu. She was very beautiful, a big girl, well built, with eyes that could start a mutiny, with cascades of black and lovely hair. By standards the European normally accepts she was quite immoral; yet by her own I do not think she was.

And she had friends. The Fifita girls lived by other standards, but Sue was always welcome in their company. She was older, and she had been good to them when they were small. It would be easy for a seaman, knowing Sue and seeing these half-dozen pretty girls in her company, to put them in the same moral category —but he would be quite wrong.

Wide-ranging writers, careless of their facts, have tagged Tahiti with the label of licentiousness; but the whalers, the traders, the explorers, and the missionaries themselves were greatly responsible for this reported licence. In certain sections of the population it always existed, but by no means did it characterize the nation.

Captain James Cook, an intelligent observer, did not make this mistake. He wrote:

Great injustice has been done the women of Otaheite and the Society Isles by those who have represented them, without exception, as ready to grant the last favour to any man who will come up to their price. But this is by no means the case; the favours of married women, and also the unmarried of the better sort, are as difficult to be obtained here as in any other country whatever. Neither can the charge be understood indiscriminately of the unmarried of the lower class, for many of these admit of no such familiarities. That there are prostitutes here, as well as in other countries, is very true, perhaps more in proportion, and such were those who came on board the ships to our people, and frequented the post we had on shore.

By seeing these mix indiscriminately with those of a different turn, even of the first rank, one is, at first, inclined to think they are all disposed the same way, and that the only difference is in the price. But the truth is the woman who becomes a prostitute does not seem, in their opinion, to have committed a crime of so deep a dye as to exclude her from the esteem and society of the community in general.

On the whole, a stranger who visits England might, with equal justice, draw the characters of the women there from those he might meet on board the ships in one of the naval ports, or in the purlieus of Covent Gardens and Drury Lane. I must, however, allow that they are all completely versed in the art of coquetry, and that very few of them fix any bounds to their conversation. It is therefore no wonder that they have obtained the character of libertines.

If there was any deterioration in this attitude over the next generation or so, it was not apparent to Moses Morrell, as he recorded in his journal of a voyage in the whale-ship *Hero,* from 1822 to 1824: "The females are very coy, and will run from a stranger if far from their huts. Others will indulge you in a few liberties. For anything further, marriage is necessary."

So thoroughly have these people absorbed the lessons taught by the European that it is difficult today to recognize this as a description of the Society Islands, centred by Tahiti. James Morrison, who was the first of any "civilized" race to stay on Tahiti for a considerable time, is a strong witness for the admirable circumspection in sexual matters attaching to the ordinary run-of-the-mill Tahitian females in the early days of contact.

In Tonga, where the European influence has been comparatively small and restricted, these standards still obtain. It is noteworthy that they seem to have been developed entirely from a decent self-respect and not from fear of consequences. Before the arrival of the European there was no risk in Polynesia of contracting disease from sexual intercourse, the female libertine lost no public respect, and the child born outside marriage was wanted and cared for; if the mother herself did not want to undertake this responsibility she found more than enough willing volunteers. A baby entailed no economic disadvantage.

Outside even this, there were circumstances in which, at least in Tahiti, infanticide was an accepted practice, even a political convenience. It was therefore common in families of rank. The practice of the community was that a man born to high rank assumed that rank immediately, thus deposing his father at birth. The father acted as regent until it pleased the incumbent to assume the duties and privileges of the title or until he was strong enough, in person or in support, to do so. Therefore a chief or a noble, the holder of a hereditary title, if he valued his position, had to postpone the establishment of a family for some years, and to this end infanticide was accepted.

So the average girl's jealous protection of her virginity developed from her regard, and the regard of her family, for that state. In days past, a virgin proudly proclaimed her condition on certain rare occasions by dancing in public, naked except for a belt about her waist and the flowers in her hair—a gesture that surely implied a challenge. It was misunderstood by all non-Polynesian witnesses; missionaries indeed were shocked, and frequently described the dance as lascivious. It was in fact the opposite, as a missionary who searched for good instead of evil would immediately have recognized.

Such a public appearance was very portentous in the life of the central figure, for Polynesian girls, as far back as history goes, have been horrified by total nudity. Today even small girls are fully dressed when they go swimming. Boys enjoy a much greater freedom. They enjoy greater freedom also in their approach to sex, with the result that the casual wooing of the Tongan is apt to be rude and abrupt. Yet the reverse of this behaviour normally attends the opening gambits of the more permanent relationships in which by far the greatest part of the population is happy.

Male freedom and the element of challenge made life something of an obstacle race for the girl who was well brought up. In these circumstances her life could be more difficult than that of her counterpart in more advanced communities, but her private successes brought their rewards; typically, she was a queen in her confidence and self-assured charm. She drew on this inner strength for her beauty. Tongan girls use and need no cosmetics, and very often their excellent taste in clothes is limited only by what is available; the garish patterns too frequently seen in the islands reflect the taste of the trader and not of the client; the Polynesian in Paris or New York buys with a sure knowledge of what is good.

Polynesian girls covered their bodies long before the European missionaries arrived, though it is true that these insatiable agents of prudery did not regard the cover as adequate. The normal dress for the woman not at work was a cover from neck to knee or from neck to ankles; for even in those days the girls preferred to have a skin as light in colour as possible, and protected it from the sun.

Sir Joseph Banks described the dress of the Tahitian women:

It must be a piece of cloth which is generally two yards wide and eleven long, is sufficient clothing for anyone, and this they put on in a thousand different ways, often very genteel. Their form of dress is, in the women, a kind of Peticoat (Parou) wrapped round their hipps and reaching about the middle of their leggs; one, two or three pieces of thick cloth about two and a half yards long and one wide (Te buta) through a hole in the middle of which they put their heads and suffer the sides of it to hang before and behind them, the open edges serving to give their arms liberty of moving; round the ends of this, as high as their wastes, are tied two or three large pieces of thin cloth, and sometimes another or two thrown over their shoulders loosely, for the rich seem to shew their greatest pride in wearing a large quantity of cloth....

It is reckoned no shame for any part of the body to be exposed to view except those which all mankind hide. . . . The women at sun set always bared their bodies down to the navel, which seemed a kind of easy undress to them as to our ladies to pull off any finery that has been used during the course of the day and change it for a loose gown and capuchin.

The cloth would not stand up to rainy weather or immersion in water, and in rain was replaced by mats, woven from tougher materials, mostly pandanus leaves. Frequently, though, the women swam naked, covering themselves as they left the water with a mat left previously in a strategic position on the beach. It was the exposure of the upper body that shocked the missionaries—on what strange psychological grounds it is difficult, in these distant days, to determine.

Modesty was a prime concern of our own sweet bevy of girls. Tokilupe and her friends Ma'ukava and Little Tupou acquired swimsuits, demure one-piece costumes so conventional that young girls in other countries might have scorned them. The Tongan girls looked charming in them. After school one day they came with Madeleine and some others past the Yellow Pier, and because I had just finished the intricate resetting of the loggerhead in the upper deck I dropped my tools and went along with them. When we got out to the deep water where the moorings bollards were, Tokilupe and Ma'ukava and Little Tupou raced for temporary concealment behind a canoe balanced at the edge of the seawall, shucked their dresses, and dived underwater fast before the suits could attract attention. They swam as most islanders do, steadily and strongly with only the head breaking water, and they kept swimming away from the shore until they were two or three hundred yards away.

The other girls, Stella and Virginia, meanwhile dived off the wharf in their clothes, the swimming-costume of most Tongan females. They didn't feel the same need to put distance between themselves and the watchers on the pier but just played and shouted near our dangling legs.

After that first time we went again, fairly often. Tokilupe contracted, as a patrol leader, to teach her Brownie troop to swim; she and her friends just threw the little ones into the water, guarded the steps against any chance of their coming out, and swam a patrol round them so they wouldn't get washed away. The lessons were swiftly effective.

There was nothing regular about these expeditions, but they were inevitable when it rained. All Tongans think of the joys of immersion when it rains. A downpour brings them out of their houses, to skip and play in the pools on the grass, to stand under the broken guttering of the house roofs, clothes and all, as under a waterfall, and to dive into the rain-lashed harbour, among the shipping. Often, when it was too wet to work on *Velata,* I went swimming with them.

7

With the work on *Velata's* hull close to completion, as
close as we could afford to bring it, we began to concentrate on making the killing gear. The heavy sisal
line, as thick as a big man's wrist, was taken down
from the palm trunks where, over the days, the playing
children had stretched it to a supple, flexible usefulness,
and was coiled carefully into a beheaded oildrum. Since
soft iron was not available, quantities of mild steel in
rod form were bought from the Government Stores and
taken to the forge presided over by Taipe, and the
manufacture of harpoons and lances began.

An element of urgency now invested the work: the
whaling season would begin at any time, and the Police
Department announced that it would issue whaling li-
cences on 10th July. Before the issue could be made,
the boat and all its furniture must stand inspection. We
needed five large sweeps, ten harpoons, ten lances,
whaling spades for cutting the meat, sailing gear in
good order, and hulls of both launch and whaler fit to
pass inspection.

In the Tongan language, the lance is *tao tamate*, the

spear that kills; the harpoon, *tao pipiki*, is the spear that clings. A child who is just ahead of the baby stage is called *pipiki*; at this development he needs little holding; set him on head or shoulders and he will cling. The name *tao pipiki* gives little indication of the deadly efficiency of the harpoon, the design of which is based on the American rather than the English type of last century (as are nearly all the world's remaining hand harpoons) but improved considerably by Tongan ingenuity.

We cut harpoon heads from crankshaft steel saved from old motor vehicles, plugs six to eight inches long, bored and channelled to take the more slender shaft of mild steel down two thirds of its length. This shaft was so pinned to the head that it would ride straight into a heavy resistance, but the least backward pull would bring the head at right angles to the shaft, and the direction of the cutting edges ensured that it could take this position easily when it was embedded in flesh. Two stops built into the design jammed the head in its new position, and helped the pin to hold the two elements of the harpoon together. When the head of the harpoon entered the flesh of the whale with the tremendous weight of the weapon behind it, it would sink deeply. Then the wooden shaft would fall away, the pull of the line would open out the harpoon head beneath the flesh, and with the head in a firm hold, the mild steel of the shaft would bend itself into fish-hook shape; so that the harpooner would have his leviathan on a fish-hook of three-eighths steel.

The length of this hook, before the whale assisted at the bending process, was four to five feet, and at the other end from the head there was a heavy metal socket with cylindrical sides. An eight-foot wooden haft fitted six inches or so into this cylinder, to make the total length of the weapon more than twelve feet. An independent rope line on the haft enabled it to be recovered after the whale was made fast—or before, if the dart missed—and the whale-line itself was bent on round the metal of the shaft.

In a modification of our own we used here about twenty feet of heavy nylon line about two and a half inches in circumference. This was to enable the harpoon to be thrown a greater distance than would be possible were the heavy sisal to be attached directly to the weapon. It had the disadvantage of limiting the distance we could pull the boat up on the fleeing whale; we could not come closer than the joint that ended this twenty feet; but since this disadvantage in length would be offset by the length of the whale behind the harpoon head, it hardly mattered. Even a baby would be more than twenty feet in length.

I was delighted here to find myself indispensable in one small capacity. The ideal hitch for the connection between iron and nylon was a rolling hitch, and I was surprised to find it unknown to such good seamen as the Tongans. It became my duty to fasten the line to the harpoon in use. Perhaps because of an exaggerated politeness—of which they were quite capable—no one except David ever learned to use this hitch while I sailed with them; and even David submitted his efforts to my inspection.

The normal gear of the whaling-men was not enough for David. It would be said, after he had caught his whale, that his was the largest and heaviest harpoon ever seen. He built a personal one especially, cutting its head from the crankshaft of the largest abandoned truck on the island.

Velata was ready for launching, the small details seemed all provided for, and the police inspection was two days away when David told me he had to go to the northern island groups, where he acted as pilot and harbour-master to overseas shipping. He would be away, he said, for about a week, superintending the comings and goings of two copra boats and a tourist ship. Meanwhile we were to get the licence without him, and whaling would be postponed.

The first whale of the season had already been caught by Cook in mid-June, operating on his licence of the previous year, the year being reckoned to the end of June. Now it was mid-July, and there was a reasonable certainty that the humpbacks would be in the area no longer than three months. The weather was excellent, but there was no guarantee that it would stay that way. My mounting excitement could not tolerate the extra days, nor, indeed, could my pocket afford them. Six other whalers were awaiting registration, and it seemed foolish to give them no competition in the early part of the season.

I had no idea how much whale-meat the Nuku'alofa market could absorb. Since the only regular source of meat supply, the Government market, never had more than a total half-ton of meat of all descriptions on the busiest days, I had the illusion that fifty or sixty tons of extra meat landed at one time might swamp the market for a short period. We were operating almost without money at this stage, and it seemed essential to put ourselves into an earning bracket without waste of time.

The more I looked at our sailing gear, the more gloomy I felt, too. It was well-kept, but on its last legs. If a whale went off with our line we had no hope whatever of replacing it. A smashed boat would mean smashed hopes; between the fourteen or fifteen of us we could not now have bought the copper nails.

But it was impossible to put any arguments in the way of David's departure. His position of pilot and harbour-master represented his only current earning-power; the tourists from America, Australia, and Europe who admired the big man on the bridge would spend more in an evening than his entire annual income; though nothing would betray the fact to them, and he would probably buy some of them drinks. His simple khaki uniform, which 'Ala would have laundered to perfection for the occasion, gave him all the standing he required. He looked a man of great substance as he marched aboard the first of his charges at Nuku'alofa. There was no indication that he had spent the previous day on the beach at his wit's end to find the materials needed to replace the centre-board box. His whole family depended on the amount he would be paid for pilotage. It was no more than £5 a day, but that was a fortune in Nuku'alofa, even though it could buy very little more than it did elsewhere.

I saw him off, sweated out the next day in the quiet desperation of a Tongan Sunday, and with my crew spent Monday night assembling the last of the whaling gear. On Monday night Tevita Uaisele and Maile Siakumi shifted the boats to Faua Harbour, where the inspection was to take place in the morning, and when they were well out in the channel, without lights in the darkness of midnight, the rudder fell off the launch. With the total indifference to disaster which is the mental state of the normal Tongan—disaster being normally at hand—they manoeuvred the heavy boat into harbour without the rudder and waited for the morning light to prepare for inspection.

No Tongan has ulcers, none has ever suffered from after effects of frustration, and I seriously question that any have ever known the degree of agitation I felt as I stood behind the police inspector and an attendant constable next morning. They examined every portable item, inspected every inch of the whaler, gave the launch a quick look-over, and carefully refrained from seeing the stripped rudder-shaft. We paid the necessary £10 licence fee and acquired the right to go whaling.

There were certain provisos, the most prominent being that the captured whale or any part thereof had to be removed ten miles from any part of Her Majesty

Queen Salote's domain within a period of twelve hours. This time was reckoned from the moment the whale was beached on the reef for cutting up, though the licence did not so stipulate. It seemed to be an inadequate period for the complete disposal of a dead whale, especially when disposal involved cutting the mass of meat into family-sized portions. I imagined at the time that the solution lay in the tolerant administration of the regulations, but my lads soon made it clear that not much leeway was ever given.

The other harbinger of the season was the burglar or burglars who paid annual attention to Tonga's powder magazine. Each year before the whalers went out there was a raid upon the island of Velitoa Hahake, where the kingdom's explosives were stored. The resident watchman would be found tied up and the magazine rifled. It had happened each year as long as anyone could remember, and the crime was generally thought to have been occasioned by the whalers' insatiable demand for gelignite.

This year the burglar was on time, the store was plundered, and from time to time mysterious visitors came in the night to offer gelignite plugs at outrageous prices. Nor were they content to sell in quantities that might have satisfied the whalers. They put minimums on their offerings; they would suggest a package deal of fifty plugs for £60, and then be alternately indignant and despondent when we refused.

Refuse we always did. I was determined to use no explosive, since I wanted to recreate the conditions of the old-time whalers as closely as possible. Most of them, from early in the nineteenth century, did use firearms, and later special whaling guns were developed, anticipating the harpoon gun and used to quieten a harpooned victim. But I wanted the whale running free on the line; I wanted the whole excitement of the primitive chase, and I was not interested in an efficiency of slaughter. Nor, though they broached the subject, was my crew wedded to the thought of gelignite capture; they were happy to try to establish a reputation for themselves with the primitive weapons.

One vendor of explosives who did not deal in quantity was a Tongan policeman who appeared with a single plug for which he asked the fantastically high price of five pounds. The first whaler to whom he made this proposition paid without a murmur, for it was of course a subtle form of blackmail, an indication that the policeman knew his victim had earlier engaged in this illicit trade.

Most of the community was under the impression that it was illegal to use gelignite on whales. Though this was not true, it was impossible in Tonga to buy gelignite from any legal source. A confusion of these two issues spread the opinion that the Tongan Parliament had legislated against the use of explosive in the hunt, and great secrecy was employed in its use.

Johnny Siola'a, joining forces with Tofa Ramsay on his fast and high-powered diesel boat 'Alaimoana, would stagger down to the boat harbour each morning wrapped in a heavy khaki greatcoat. Though he was an athletic type, he was helped aboard by two crew members who exercised extreme care and who accompanied Johnny to the stern, where he divested himself of his unaccustomed garment (even on rainy days) and laid it tenderly within a chest which he immediately padlocked.

On returning to Fa'ua Harbour after a day at sea the actors in the comedy reversed the procedure. Johnny, fresh, most likely, from prodigies of activity, would unlock the depository, lift the old greatcoat with loving care, and accept the solicitous assistance of his two seamen-turned-valets in putting it on. Then he would walk carefully along the deck, disembark as awkwardly as an ancient politician paying an unaccustomed duty

96

call on island voters, and walk steadily to his home. All motor traffic gave him a wide berth.

Perhaps there were legal ways of obtaining explosives, and certainly, if there were, these seamen would know them, for they thought little of running a few hundred miles, and several had been frequent visitors to Fiji, Samoa, and New Zealand. The quantities taken in the annual burglary seemed more than sufficient for the comparatively meagre needs of the whalers, but there were other illegal usages, particularly in the supply of sea fish to a number of the town and village markets.

By far the greater quantity of stolen explosives was not taken in the annual spectacular on Velitoa Hahake. It was collected, stick by stick, from the normal blasting operations of the kingdom. Perhaps three plugs would be inserted in a hole drilled for five, and the other two, subtly concealed until the thief was off the site, went on the thriving blackmarket. In underwater blasting even greater quantities were recovered by the local grafters. The practitioners developed a high degree of efficiency with minimal charges, with such consistency that several of the engineers in charge must have revised their estimates of the amount of explosive necessary for all manner of clearing and levelling jobs in the local coral.

The prospect of a new harbour designed for Nuku'alofa was at this time lightening the hearts of the gelignite kings. They could see an endless supply of gelignite made available. My impression was that the annual burglary was an institution designed to cover up the wholesale nobbling that went on all through the year. That would be a master-touch calculated to delight the scheming and devious minds behind the racket.

Since David was not expected to return until the following Tuesday, and we were now under the necessity of fitting a new plate rudder to the launch, Tevita Uai-sele, as second-in-command, and Ve'etutu Pahulu, as sailing-master, decided to open the season with a picnic at which all the workers, all the children, all the wives, and all the legitimate girlfriends could let their hair down and celebrate.

But the altered schedule of one of the copra boats brought David back four days early. He approved the picnic arrangements for the following Monday, but since we all felt that the intervening time should not now be wasted, he proposed that we attend to the most important preliminary on our programme, a deferential thanks-offering to Queen Salote.

This was to be combined with a peculiarly Tongan duty of my own. A year before, in Auckland, New Zealand, the Queen's grandson, Taufa'ahau, a six-foot-four-inch stripling of fifteen years, had honoured me with a Tongan name. He was presiding at a kava ring held in honour of the Minerva Reef survivors, and the name conferred certain privileges and duties of rank. It made me a *matapule,* one of the appointed aristocracy of Tonga drawn from the ranks of prominent commoners. It also gave me the appreciated name of Manusiu oe Pasifiki, recognizing my literary endeavours by likening me to the frigate bird that ranges the wide Pacific picking up titbits.

Any of the Tongan nobles can appoint *matapules* though they are limited to one or two nominations. The rank follows rather closely the old conventions of English knighthood, and the relationship of a *matapule* to his chief is similar to that of the squire to his knight, though there are important differences. For one thing, the *matapule* can use the property of his principal as his own; he can talk to his principal in a forthright fashion that would not be acceptable from anyone else, and what he says in public ceremony is attributed to his principal.

98

The rank of the *matapule* is determined by the degree of eminence of the man who has appointed him, and this becomes a very important matter, since a *matapule* must preside at most of the important functions of Tongan life and normally must give up his place to another *matapule* who outranks him. Since I had been appointed by royalty my degree of eminence was high —an embarrassment, for I knew nothing of my duties and could not speak the language beyond a useful word or two. Moreover, though a royal person may appoint, within reason, as many *matapules* as he likes, I was the first named by young Taufa'ahau and, had I been Tongan, would have taken precedence over succeeding ones.

I was greatly appreciative of my appointment, but by right I should have made a gesture of acceptance; I should have slaughtered a large pig and cooked it myself as the central dish of a feast; I should have invited Queen Salote to the feast and otherwise indicated my great pleasure at the honour conferred upon me.

The Tongan of any authority is, by training and environment, equipped to handle the long and complicated ceremonious procedures which this would entail, but I felt inadequate, though I was more than willing to play my part. David now suggested that since I was a fisherman and proposed to fish whale in Tonga—since, also, my Tongan name was of the sea—certain modifications of the programme suitable to the privileged status of the seaman would be in order. I should take *Velata* to the drift grounds, supervise the capture of a freight of fish and, returning to Nuku'alofa, take the whole freight to the palace, a gift to the Queen.

The suitability of this was enhanced by the identity of the little ship herself. *Velata* was the name of the principal fort of the first Taufa'ahau, from which he conquered and unified the components of the Tongan group. It was in Ha'apai, whence Taufa'ahau came, and our men were principally from that group. Significant was my naming by the current Taufa'ahau. "Velata" was a greatly honoured name in Tonga especially for its royal connections, and it seemed appropriate that the reconstituted *Velata's* first catch should go in its entirety to the Queen.

Shortly before dark on Friday, therefore, we set out for the drift grounds of Hakau Mama'o, far to the north of Nuku'alofa. Long after dark we saw the headlights of a vessel heading back to port. She was far on the distant horizon, but Sioeli's eyes danced with excitement.

"Tofua'a, tofua'a," he insisted; but it was more than thirty minutes before we passed, recognized the *'Alaimoana*, and saw that she did indeed have a moderately large humpback in tow. Then the calculations began. It was the fortnightly Government payday, which indicated ample money for buying meat. It was a Saturday, which meant that everyone would have the time, not only to buy, but to prepare the earth ovens. There had been no whale meat on the market for a month. Everyone agreed that the capture augured a great season.

I listened to the talk, David translating here and there, but my thoughts were with the great bulk of the whale, fastened head and back-fin to the little launch, a quarter of its weight. We passed it at a distance of about a hundred yards; it was hardly to be identified in the dark night, but a riding-light lifted slivers of silver from the contours of the shining black hide, the *'Alaimoana* wallowed and pitched, tethered to its victim, whose great tired head seemed to strain for reunification with the depths. It was hard to see in the dark night; what we identified was the effect of the tow upon the captor tug, and we filled in the blanks from flashes of reflected light, hardly to be distinguished from the reflections of the water surface. It was the first whale victim I had seen, and I was wholly seized with the concept of the impertinence of man, a dust-mote on an ocean who believes himself a god and assumes a theomorphic mantle.

Tofa Ramsay with his whale represented the changing era, come late to Tonga. His *'Alaimoana* had enough speed to outrun a humpback and therefore his tactics approached those of the industrial whale-catchers of the Antarctic. He would hurry and harry a whale, sometimes firing at it, until it took an unwise refuge in direct flight, its breathing periods coming closer and closer together and its appearances more predictable. The homemade harpoon bomb would finish it, but if the explosive charge was too large or too near the skin on detonation, the animal would sink, irrecoverably.

When, about midnight, we came to the drift grounds, I was tired, and the excitements arising from our mission and from the near-encounter with the successful whaler had left me feeling flat. I lay down and was asleep within minutes. I was vaguely aware of much shifting of our position throughout the night, and in my sleep rightly equated this with unsuccessful fishing, so that when I awoke three or four hours later I was disappointed, though not surprised, to find that not enough fish had been caught to provide a decent meal, let alone a gift fit for a queen.

Sioeli passed me a line to which I snoozed two hooks and a sinker. It had hardly touched bottom, at about thirty fathoms, when the baits were taken one after the other, and I brought in two splendid fish of the variety the Tongans call "koango", the best line of the night and an excellent one at any time. I had my line bottomed again before I realized that my companions were deeply impressed, and why. It was a superstitious reaction: koango was the Queen's favourite fish, and no other fisherman had caught any. Then I had slept until, apparently, the koango were ready for my line.

This was hardly borne in on me when I caught another fish, a maunga. This type of drift fishing is called *tao maunga*. Though other fish may be caught in greater quantity, the maunga gives his name to the avocation. So the moment I boated this one I coiled my line and went back to bed, feeling it was best for me to straddle firmly the reputation I had established in two lucky casts. As a reputation it was little deserved, but I felt I could use it with profit. In the next five minutes I blotted the bright sketch of an efficient fisherman by being sea-sick; it was many years since I had spent the night in a fishing-boat on a sea that was by no means calm, but I laid partial blame on an excitement conjured up from metaphysical as well as more familiar sources.

We returned home with what turned out to be a catch only just within the bounds of respectability, packed it in baskets plaited of new green coconut leaves, spruced ourselves up, and took it to the palace. It is the privilege of every Tongan to call at the palace whenever he feels like it, and he is not self-conscious about it at all. He makes the most elaborate preparations, though. He takes a most patriotic joy in exercising these rights; the republican can never begin to know the joy a monarchy affords its adherents, for the Queen, after all, is the representative of her people, not elected in some capricious political backswing, but trained from birth to the position and the responsibility.

We were unfortunate, this day, in that Queen Salote, under medical treatment for a broken bone in her foot, was confined to her bed. She was, in fact, asleep; and we were entertained in her absence by one of her *matapules,* Ma'ufualu, whose blood is Fijian. Like other *matapules* appointed directly by the Queen, he could never wear European-type dress again; he must always wear the *vala* and *ta'ovala* which a Tongan dons for all important and most unimportant occasions. He made a gracious acceptance of our gift.

Meantime, Tofa Ramsay had been selling his whale on the beach. It was a well-grown cow, forty-six feet long, and it had been stranded on the reef a scant half-mile from the town. From early light there had been a procession of people wading out to it to buy the meat. They grumbled, for Tofa charged them a high price—two or three pence a pound instead of the more usual penny—and so they did not buy as heavily as usual. By nightfall he had taken about £820, but a good deal of the whale was left on the beach, and at first light on Monday he had to tow it to sea. His licence would have required him to shift it earlier, but the Sunday observance laws gave him a spell after the strenuous work of cutting and selling.

In my absence Ve'etutu took Madeleine to see the whale. He took her out in a dinghy and rowed between the great mounds of meat, over water red with blood, between the blood-stained butchers dropping with weariness, the people standing up to their necks in the sea, standing in line to buy the meat. Away to the eastward, microscopic particles of blubber floating on the water gave it an unbelievable clarity; you could see the bottom at forty feet where the blubber-slick marked the water. I had thought that the water would boil with sharks where the rivers of blood among the waiting people discoloured it; and though I was told that sharks often do attend the distribution of the meat, on this day there were none.

The smell of blubber, faint but penetrating, rose over the town; backyards filled with smoke sifting through the slanted sun beneath the coconuts as the earth ovens were set; the roads dotted with horse-drawn drays taking slabs of whale-meat home to village communities;

and the deep content engendered by superfluity seemed to pervade the whole of Tongatapu.

The girls danced for us that night, as on most nights when I was home, swaying gracefully one after another in the story-choreography of the *tau'olunga*, a dance which in displaying all the correlated movements of all the muscles, but especially those of the hands and arms, seems to me to outclass the hula by far.

Tu'imala, sitting near us on the mats, called for Liola to dance, and Liola, twelve years old, plump and pretty but painfully shy, came in at last to the insistence of rhythmic clapping, executed no more than two or three steps, then ran away. There was silence for just a moment, almost a shocked silence; then Tu'imala rose to her feet and danced, the same feet, the same hands and arms that danced for Queen Elizabeth in Tonga's culminating tribute of beauty. Everyone sat breathless. Though Tu'imala's performance on this occasion was inferior to what it had been at the peak of her perfection, I doubt that she had ever been accorded a more genuine attention or a more heartfelt final acclamation. Five days later, in the Nuku'alofa Hospital, she gave birth to a fine healthy eleven-pound baby boy, well over his time. It was then that I realized the extent of her gesture, though her condition of course had been obvious. She had felt that she owed us the dance because of Liola's defection; only very young Tongan girls, and very shy, will dodge the pleasant duty of dancing for a guest.

Tongans have always put their women on pedestals. In those islands it is the function of the female to be decorative and charming, to sing and dance, to lift life above the level of the commonplace.

Herman Melville, an accurate observer, noted as a peculiarity of the Marquesans conditions that still obtain in the Friendly Islands:

104

Nowhere are the ladies more assiduously courted; nowhere are they better appreciated as the contributors to our highest enjoyment, and nowhere are they more sensible of their powers. . . . The gentle sex in the valley of Typee were exempt from toil. . . . Their light household occupations, together with the manufacture of tappa, the platting of mats, the polishing of drinking-vessels, were the only employments pertaining to the women. And even these resembled those pleasant avocations which fill up the elegant morning leisure of our fashionable ladies at home.

So, on the Monday, after a day of rest that was intolerably drawn out over a period in which my mounting excitement and the imagined worries of unforeseeable disaster allowed me little recreation, every whaling-man brought his wife or his girlfriend and his daughters, and with picnic viands of live pigs, live chickens, and sweet potatoes we sailed for one of the dozen *motus,* the sandy coral islands, in Nuku'alofa Harbour.

Ahead of us, on the horizon, *'Alaimoana* and a smaller assisting vessel struggled and strained to the outer ocean. Their task was to dispose of the bones, the hide, and the intestines of the whale; had their meat been lower-priced, so I was told, they could have avoided having to put to sea with this residue. Even the intestines of the whale can be eaten; for the humpback, by the time he reaches Tonga, has had no meal for something like two months; each draws the ingredients of his energy, and each cow her vast milk supply as well, from the huge store of their bulk.

A string band played, and the girls danced the narrow decks as *Velata* leaned to the trade wind. The leaping song followed the patterns of leaping waves. To me the ocean puts its own seal of reality on emotional situations; and on this day, in this company, the emotion was happiness, so strong and so cleansing that I forgot to be apprehensive of the possibility that our conflict with the whale would come to nothing.

We ferried to and from the shore with outriggers based on the otherwise empty island, an island crowned with the heads of coconuts grown haphazard. The men gathered and opened a score or more of the nuts and grated the white meat against the newly trimmed edge of a dead branch and later expressed a gallon of cream from the mound of gratings; they put the cream with the chicken meat in banana-leaf bags for baking in the earth oven, and spitted the pigs and peeled the tapioca roots; they chopped the firewood and gathered the stones for the oven and cleared resting-places in the green bush and dug the oven-hole. The girls made garlands or swam and danced, singing the while, or ranged the bush for scented flowers and leaves, and dived for bêche-de-mer.

The meal, made and served without benefit of a single plate or pot, without a single utensil not growing in the bush, was so delicious that the most prosaic description here, if accurate, would only foster unbelief. And in the afternoon there was dancing on the sand, and games and races, and swimming in the shallows, and towards the night we sailed back home, festooned, each one of us, with the green and gold and yellow tendrils of *fatai*, which grows only by the seaside, so that everyone seeing us would know how we had been spending our day.

8

Overnight the weather worsened, and we began our whaling on a day of unseasonable squalls: high gusts of cold wind playing between the awkward limits of twenty to thirty knots, so that our tender canvas, reefed to usable limits, was yet subjected to a dangerous strain. The skies were grey and driving, the rain beat cold through out shirts.

A half-mile to port, *Kaimoana* strained and chugged, George Fifita, a jack-of-all-trades, at the wheel and, as lookouts, Sifa Veafeki, a taxi-driver with a yen for adventure, Feteleni Sekona, a relation of Finau Laione's and a very American-looking Sonny Vincent, who answered to the name "Papalangi", meaning "European". Sonny (he spelt it "Sani") was the child of an American serviceman who had been stationed in Tonga twenty-two years before, and he didn't possess a single Tongan feature. He didn't have more than three or four English words, and he used these to ask all likely looking strangers whether they had ever seen the State of Iowa. He was a tall, athletic-looking lad. His seamanship, like Feteleni's, was non-existent, and Sifa's was not well developed, but

107

they could be expected to follow George Fifita's commands and keep a good lookout for whale.

In *Velata* there was a much more likely looking company: David, Maile, Ve'etutu, Sioeli, Finau, Tevita Uaisele, William Fa, Teiapa'a Bloomfield, Roger Bath, with whom I had arranged to take photographs of the whaling, and myself. On the previous night we had temporarily lost Fine Feuiaki. His mother died and he had to take the first boat to Ha'apai. His place was taken by Olive Pooi, from the blacksmith shop. The only Tongans less than expert were young Finau Laione and Teiapa'a Bloomfield. Teiapa'a had elected himself to the care of the lance. He wore his life-jacket —the only one we carried—at all times, and at the slightest alarm leaped to the thwarts and grasped the lance.

In the first hour of daylight we saw the launch signal a whale-sighting. We raced downwind in the direction indicated, and caught a brief glimpse of a black bulk at a great distance and travelling into wind. There was no hope of coming up with it, and we resumed our patrol.

In the heavy weather the jaws of the boom broke, and in early afternoon we headed for the small island of Atata to make repairs. Something under a mile in length, and a few hundred yards wide, the island sheltered a dozen families, mostly of Ha'apai origin, islanders who could not forego the island life yet liked to live close to the capital.

Our men took ashore a bush-knife and a hatchet, a file and an oilstone, and with these tools cut new jaws for the boom. They chose the timber from among the naturally bent branches of two ancient specimens of the paper hibiscus, a tree that furnishes timbers of varying qualities for different usages; and they trimmed and finished the carpentry by eye.

When it came to the removal of the old jaws they found the oregon of the boom rotted beneath. From one of the houses someone produced a short length of oregon pine, carefully harboured against some such emergency and, still working with the bush-knife, they cut the boom, prepared long angled surfaces and spliced the new length of oregon in. The whole job took about five hours. Since the number and nature of the tools stipulated that no more than two men could work at one time, this compared very favourably with the time a modern boatshed would allot. And the chosen timber was probably of better quality than could be bought. The practical demonstration of a true seaman's understanding of bush materials was not new to me, but I was impressed anew. There were bolts available from the old job to fasten the jaws, but the splices in the boom were seized with nylon fishing-line. In the next three months, under heavy and sometimes violent use, the repairs did not let us down.

While the carpentry went on, some of it in pouring rain, we were entertained by the Atata islanders, who sacrificed a pig to our comfort. And after we had feasted we were given the use of a hut, built after the fashion that was ancient before the first Dutchman ever raised a Tongan landfall, with curving bows beautifully patterned against the splayed rafters in the rounded ends of the house, and an entrance at each of the four points of the compass. Apart from the mats on the floor, the only furniture in the house was an enormous iron-framed feather-bed, which was put at my disposal while the others made sleeping places on the floor. In the early light, before the small community was awake, we put to sea again, a little happier with our strengthened gear.

All the following day we worked west, against the blustering south-east wind, and anchored that night under the shelter of an island called Tau, a name that means "to arrive", for it is the northern outlier of the Tonga tapu group.

So we worked back and forth all that week and saw no whales; saw little, indeed, in the poor visibility of the grey drift of low and racing clouds, in the stinging face of the rain. Our search ended each day at about two o'clock in the afternoon; it is accepted among whalers that after that hour there is small chance of catching a whale lazy or basking at the surface; he is alive and lively, and may as well be left alone.

Friday had to end our fishing for the week. A whale caught on Saturday could not be used because of the Sunday observance laws; and towards noon on Friday we were already positioning ourselves to make an easy run home from the west. The weather was heavy, the seas raising themselves higher than I had seen them thereabouts, so that I was reminded of the note that Captain Bligh made of his condition in these waters on the first day of his open-boat voyage after the mutiny on the *Bounty*. As recorded by Sir John Barrow:

> At daybreak . . . the forlorn and almost hopeless navigators saw with alarm the sun to rise fiery and red—a sure indication of a severe gale of wind; and accordingly, at eight o'clock it blew a violent storm, and the sea ran so very high that the sail was becalmed when between the seas, and too much to have set when on top of the sea; yet it is stated that they could not venture to take it in, as they were in very imminent danger and distress, the sea curling over the stern of the boat and obliging them to bale with all their might.

Ours was not nearly so extreme a case for our open boat was much larger than Bligh's and our crew only two-thirds of his in number; but the experience of the seas cutting the wind from the sail was similar, and at times frightening. Towards lunchtime we split the sail.

We were then near enough to a line of reef to work

our way behind it, and did so, signalling *Kaimoana* at the same time to come in, since she carried our needles and thread, and canvas for repair. The size of the seas, however, convinced *Kaimoana's* unseasoned crew that she was in some danger; she was rolling through an arc of not less than sixty degrees, thirty and more from the vertical; and rolling violently, as we could see from *Velata*. They had no desire to work across the seas to our vicinity, and instead they cut and ran for the port.

We were then put to the necessity of contriving repairs to the sail, without needles, without thread, and without spare canvas—a situation over which these whalers didn't waste a moment in idleness, even while there was still a slim chance that *Kaimoana* was just making her way round the quieter end of the reef. William Fa, who proved to have the strongest underwear, contributed it as cover for the split, which was fortunately small. A variety of needles was effected from nails of various sizes sharpened on the oilstone, from fishhooks straightened and filed, and from doubled-over fishing traces. Thread was recovered from a torn tarpaulin. Half a dozen hands kept materials tolerably stretched. The mend that we put in that day, backed with stronger canvas when we got to port, was still doing duty at the end of the season.

The mend cost us five hours. A changing wind converted our homeward way into a long beat, and after dark the wind dropped away. Ashore, a minor panic developed, beginning when three Tongans called at Roger Bath's ketch in Faua Harbour, and wordlessly, for they had no English, delivered to Roger's wife a box containing all Roger's things including a pipe from which he was seldom separated.

Those who saw the *Kaimoana* crew had little doubt that they had been through some shattering experience. Questioned, they told the truth: they hadn't seen us for some hours, and it had been rough when they left us.

Somehow, through the usual agencies perhaps, this was mistranslated and word got around that they hadn't seen us for three days. One of the Bath boys came to Madeleine with the news; she took a taxi to the ketch to discover that the harbour-master had sent out radios to shipping.

The minor panic might have become a major one except for David's brother Laitia, who was worried about the effect all this speculation might have on David's reputation. He took command and said he'd conduct a search himself, but he'd leave it till four o'clock in the morning.

His choice of time was a shrewd and typically Tongan move. By that time the tide would have ebbed to such a degree that only one channel would give access to the harbour, even for a small boat, and there would be no chance of his missing us. It happened even as he said. In the inner harbour the sea was calm, the wind had dropped to such a degree that I had let everyone else go to sleep—for they were worn out—taken the tiller myself, and was bringing *Velata* home at a speed of something under a knot. We met Laitia about five miles out and were happy to take a towrope. It was broad daylight when we reached the house and set all the worries to rest.

From this adventure, or from the wind-rocked week preceding, I half-expected a torture of assaulted muscles and sedentary years insulted; for, with brief interludes of a joyous sanity, I had spent years away from the ocean. But the punishment I deserved for this period of neglect was averted by the magic of small Tongan fingers.

Every observer of the Polynesian way of life has commented on the many varieties of massage to which the influential male submits his muscles, and now I was to learn the benefits for myself. Every day when I was home from the sea I laid myself full-length on the mats to submit to the attentions of the masseurs.

They came in numbers up to eight; there was no room for more to work. Two at each leg, one at each arm, one at my chest, and one at my head, they worked on me for an hour at a time, the most efficient and most delightful of rejuvenating agencies any man ever knew. Mostly they were the young girls, Stella and Tokilupe and Virginia, and their friends, Little Tupou and Liola. Very often 'Ala or one of the elder women supervised the process, but there was no restriction on age; nearly always one or two children were in the group, learning an art that is of prime importance. Kalo was little more than two years old, and her tiny fingers searched and probed the muscles of my hand and forearm; even at that age they had some indefinable power, some strength too, beneath the gossamer touch.

There was no restriction on sex either; Fifita or Hopoate or some of the younger lads sometimes sat in and massaged, and their touch was sure and firm, though none of the lads I knew had quite the same power in their fingers as the girls. Ve'etutu and Laitia, among the men, quite frequently undertook my massage by themselves; they tended to use lashings of oil and a great outpouring of energy, but the physical and probably the psychological benefits no more than matched those given by the teams of girls.

Requisites for the patient were faith and a capacity for relaxation—characteristics not unallied. I saw several Europeans, fired perhaps by my example, submit aches and pains to the ministering fingers of these masseurs; few of them were patient for more than a minute or so, and a great many actively disliked the sensations. With my head in Tokilupe's lap I would feel the balls of her thumbs close down on my eyeballs with such direct pressure that I could hardly resist a cry, or the ten digital pads search deep to the crevices of my skull, skirting nerve centres at the back of the jawbones and behind my ears.

There were moments in my early experience when I was tempted to call off the process, but I was glad that I never did. I would experience a release from the reality of the present allied to sleep; indeed I sometimes confused the condition with sleep, but it was a sleep in which the capacity for enjoyment was not stilled. There was a sensual pleasure combined with the well-being of calm, as though my muscles had come into harbour after the battering of a storm. The aromatic oils delighted me, the ministrations of eighty fingers conjured me to a happy relaxation.

I found other uses for massage: when I had a headache, for example. All my life I have occasionally suffered from headaches for which I had never before found the remedy. I found it now in the fingertips of children, if I could follow their treatment with a night of sleep. They eased strained muscles and tired feet. They could massage me to wakefulness or to sleep. They could ease the blue moods; indeed our continuing failure to come to grips with the whale I needed sent me oftener to their aid. They had a dozen forms of massage, all of them worked out with a very close knowledge of practical anatomy. They massaged with the fingertips, with the base of the hand, with the point of the elbows, with the round of a short rod, with a vessel filled with hot water, with a copious flow of oil or a minimum of this necessary lubrication.

Sometimes David would come home and throw himself down on the mats, and one of the children, Tokilupe or Fifita, would walk about on his broad back, using for locomotion only the elbow and knee points of angled limbs. The rhythm of pressures here was severe. Perhaps the Tongan understanding of anatomy and the needs of the body contributed to the excellent physique

114

they achieved on what always seemed to me an inadequate diet.

In the following week the weather held unseasonably stormy, so bad that at times, if the position were vacant, we abandoned our cruise along the deeper waters where we could reasonably be expected to intercept the northbound whales, and took our vessels to a minute haven of quiet refuge among the boiling reefs of the island of Malinoa. It was a tiny island, of perhaps half an acre, and its advantage to us derived from its being the site of a lighthouse, the top of which soared above the level of the coconut heads and afforded us a lookout platform from which we could see many square miles of ocean. With a lookout in the wind-wrenched eyrie of the light's platform, and another one or two men in pandanus trees, we could lie down and relax and dream of whales. The lookout was usually Lau'ia. He had eyes that fastened upon minute detail, and an intensity of purpose which held him unrelaxed to the task of watching.

At the base of the sand-spit that pointed towards the south-east and Nuku'alofa was a huge *puko-lea* tree, a Hernandia. The Tongan name means "it grows and talks", and the great size of the tree, where it is found, testifies to the first part of the name. In the larger sense it is also true that it talks; in the relevant legend it spoke to lost voyagers landed on an island where they could find no sustenance, and it said, "Take me and eat." As long as the legends are remembered people will know that the *puko-lea* promises the preservation of life; the leaves can be eaten baked, boiled or raw, and they are nutritious as cabbage, and effective too in the treatment of scurvy. No child fails to ask why the tree got its name.

Tongans show no great attachment to the food the Hernandia provides, but because of the legend it is the most effective emergency ration of the Pacific.

Beneath the great tree on Malinoa there was a line of six graves, two or three marked with coral grave-stones, and on two of these names had been roughly scratched. On this deserted island, affording only a temporary refuge, the graves looked out of place. I thought them of recent origin, for they were well kept, with fresh white sand spread over the weedless site and raked into a smooth surface, but Sioeli, who had led me there, told me their story. He had come almost at a run, so eager was he to let me know it.

"These men were executed, Olefi. They were shot by the King's guard, oh, a long time ago. Seventy years and more. They tried to kill a man who was very much hated, but they failed, and I can't think so great a punishment could be deserved. A man can be a great rogue and earn less punishment, and these were not rogues. They were good men."

The immaculate condition of the graves, so difficult of access, proved that others beside Sioeli thought the punishment excessive.

In theory, capital punishment is still a possibility in Tonga, but the Queen believes that the rule of a woman should result in no punishments so harsh; that justice must be tempered, in a female reign, with more mercy than perhaps a man might show; and there have been no hangings in her time.

The intended victim of the six men lying in Malinoa's mass grave was a Wesleyan missionary, the Reverend Shirley Baker, a man who at one stage seemed as though he might become the actual ruler of Tonga. A statue in Ha'apai commemorates him; but the condition of the Malinoa graves testifies that his name would not in any event have been forgotten.

Baker, a Londoner ordained in Australia as a Wesleyan clergyman, went to Tonga in 1860 and immediately, according to the *Memoirs* written by two of his daughters, found: "While the Mission had been most

116

successful in spiritual matters, yet . . . nothing had been done to raise the Tongans up a nation. He very soon manifested the deepest interest in the political, social and physical—besides the spiritual—well-being of the Tongans."

He determined, they recorded, that his life work should be the moulding of Tongans into a nation independent and self-supporting, though indeed a similar condition obtained before his arrival. To his stated end, he embarked upon a temporal career that at times showed little conformity with the principles he must have preached from his Nuku'alofa pulpit. He built a magnificent house for himself, and ordered from New Zealand the materials for a royal palace for Taufa'ahau. Because of his influence in secular matters the Wesleyan Conference recalled him to New Zealand in 1879. In the following year 'Unga, the King's son and Prime Minister of the Kingdom, went to Auckland for his health and died there. Shirley Baker must have seen fate beckon; he accompanied the body back to Tonga, and the King invited him to become Prime Minister in 'Unga's place. He retired from the church, and shortly afterwards a free and independent Church of Tonga arose, attracting the King and most of the adherents of the earlier Wesleyan foundation. From this time there was a savage persecution, physical and administrative, of those who did not make the changeover.

The King was eighty-three years old. Shirley Baker rapidly demonstrated that he had a comprehensive influence over the old man, and rose to a position in which he held or controlled most of the portfolios of the Cabinet. While he was thus dominant the most savage and vicious punishments, involving protracted tortures, were inflicted on anyone who broke the laws. Even the courts came under Baker's direct influence. The ancient deference to women came under attack. Rank did not protect those whom Baker branded as

117

transgressors, neither did any consideration of humanity.

The evening of 13th January 1887 saw the tension between repression and reaction rise to breaking pitch. Baker had been home for dinner and was driving back the the Government offices accompanied by his son Shirley and his daughter Lillian. The children were sitting behind their father, who was driving, when, as the girls wrote in the *Memoirs,* the calm and happiness of the moment was shattered:

On a lonely part of the road, the horse was going at a spanking pace when suddenly it shied at a native who burst out from the bushes and stood squarely in front of the trap. The native pulled out a gun, raised it . . . and hesitated for a moment.

Dragging the horse to a standstill, Dr Baker began to climb out of the trap, but his son, who had already jumped out, shouted a warning, and bravely ordered the man to put down his gun. Three other men appeared, then the native fired twice aiming at Dr Baker and his son at almost point-blank range. In that instant Miss Baker flung herself in front of her father, throwing her arms around his neck. She fell shot through the thigh. Dr Baker's son was wounded in the arm, the heavy bullet smashing the bone to pieces. The horse bolted, crashing into the swooning daughter and throwing her to the ground, badly damaging her spine.

The four men were named Fehoko, Latui, Naisa, and Isaiah. Baker also claimed to have seen a man and a woman standing a bit farther off; they were Lavuso and his wife, two who had been pressed into service more or less at gun-point by the others.

For some reason the attempt collapsed at this point. The man who had apparently master-minded the af-

fair, Tobui, a minor chief with lands at Mu'a and Ho-
longa, immediately tried to gather a force to raise re-
bellion, but his followers, overawed by the Government
action, surrendered him at Mu'a on 15th January.

Eleven days later the trials took place, Shirley Baker
himself acting as prosecutor. Here the prisoners
claimed that George Tuku'aho was behind the attempt.
This was not proved. Twelve accused were found
guilty. Eleven were sentenced to death and the other to
penal servitude for twenty-one years. Five of the prisoners were then pardoned.

The remaining six, on the day after the close of the
trial, were taken aboard a vessel to Malinoa, where a
firing-party of fifty men, all from the two northern
groups and therefore unrelated to the conspirators, shot
them one at a time. Tobui saw his son Motuhi shot,
then refused a blindfold. The others were shot in the
back; Tobui's last request was that he be permitted to
face the rifle barrels. They must have barked at point-
blank range; from the foot of the grave to the bank
where the firing-party was ranked is not more than fifteen yards at the outside.

But if George Tuku'aho was involved, and if his object had been to take over the country, he was to learn
that there are subtler and more fortuitous ways. When
Shirley Baker was retired from the Prime Ministry,
Tuku'aho was his successor. His son, Viliame Tungi,
became the husband of Queen Salote, and his grand-
sons or their heirs will occupy the throne.

What is the secret of the tended graves? No one
could tell me. Perhaps they did not want to.

"We think a lot about these men," Sioeli said. "We
often think how hard it was that so many should die
because two children lay wounded."

The revolution achieved a purpose. In fear or in re-
venge, Baker, acting in the name of the aged and infirm
King, instituted a persecution of the diehard Wes-

leyans so intense that complaints came to the British High Commissioner for the Western Pacific, Sir Charles Mitchell. His gentle solutions—amnesty for acts done during the disturbances, future freedom of worship—made him a target for Baker; and his successor, Sir John Thurston, after a further inquiry, had Baker deported.

Two years later Baker returned to Ha'apai as an Anglican missionary, having secured a licence from a New Zealand bishop, but he lived only another year or so. Lillian was crippled all her life. She lived on in Ha'apai, attended by her sister, who established a fine reputation in the Ha'apai community as a nurse.

The black gravestones beneath the Talking Tree look as though they were set up only yesterday. They too are eloquent; the Tongan is vividly aware of his freedom, and since that time no outsider has assumed any position of leadership within the framework of government.

When we walked back to the sand beneath the lighthouse, Finau Laione was playing with two snakes, each between three and four feet long, banded black and sulphur-yellow, with yellow bellies. He held them by their flattened tails, and they swayed gently back and forth, striking feebly at his legs. Sioeli laughed.

"There was one time, on picnics, we all used to play with snakes, Olefi," he said. "But about ten years ago there was a Danish ship here, an expedition concerned with the sea. Some of the crew, or some scientists they had, saw the children playing with the snakes and told us they were venomous. Since then hardly anyone plays with snakes any more. We knew they could kill dogs; they very often kill dogs; but we didn't know, until those Danes told us, that they could kill people."

The banded sea-snake is venomous and would kill swiftly indeed, but his mouth opens so narrowly and his teeth are so far back from the opening that a flat surface, the surface of a human leg, for instance, as Finau was demonstrating seems to fox him. If he were to strike at a finger, or the narrow fold of skin between finger and thumb, the blow might be, from his point of view, successful; the rounded leg of a dog, the narrower parts available on nose and ears, are vulnerable points.

On Malinoa, alone among the *motus* of Tongatapu, the sea-snakes come for holidays from the water. They are always there, resting in hollows beneath the trees, stretched out in crannies away from the light, enjoying the dryness. I learnt to draw them out of hiding and take them to the beach and release them to the sea; rather, I taught myself, for the others ignored the snakes and some actively disliked them. But I felt better when I knew that the snakes had taken to the sea. They were warm to the touch, and the skin felt tough. I wondered that the Tongans did not eat them; they are good food, much like chicken, but Tongans shrink from the idea. They will not eat lizard either, and they show what seems to be an associated repugnance when faced with mushrooms or any other edible fungi. Yet connoisseurs of these items will sometimes recoil from elements of the Tongan diet, like octopus and beche-de-mer. The snakes too, would provide valued leather for belts and hatbands. Tongans, strangely enough, do not think so.

When Finau had finished playing with the snakes he let them go into the sea and turned his attention to crabs, the little ghost crabs that ran around the beach. He caught them and crammed them into his mouth, crunching them while their legs still raced in the motions of scrambling away. I have seen Ve'etutu do the same thing with a large, harder crab, the size of the palm of his hand, and wondered that the inside of his mouth escaped undamaged.

Finau could play with death on the island. Only one man, William Fa, had been in worse case than Finau on Minerva Reef. At the time of rescue William had been unable to walk, hardly able to move and for weeks after was fed intravenously. He had collapsed some twenty or thirty days before rescue while wading thigh-deep on the reef in order to spear fish. Paralysed, he had fallen into the water at a difficult moment while he and Fine Feuiaki were being dogged by an eight-foot shark. Fine had speared the shark, though he too stood on the quicksand edge of death, and dragged shark and William, spear and freight of fish back to their shelter on a wreck.

William had regained his strength. He was sturdily built now with massive shoulders that seemed like a carapace perched upon the columns of his triceps muscles. He was shy, had little English, and frequently went away by himself, though not from surliness, for the sweet shy smile that lit his pockmarked face was born of a sincere good-humour.

While Finau played, William combed the coverts of the little island. When he found a sprouting coconut he planted it. He cleared away the growth from the weaker food plants so that they might flourish, and once, when a heavy banana sprout, still fresh, was thrown up on the island beach in a storm, he took it inland a little way and planted it; and when I last saw it it had life.

William would never forget the starvation on Minerva Reef. When food was divided up he would frequently hide a portion. Or he would take his share to a place where he could eat it by himself. He hoarded water and food; he will do so, I imagine, all his life. And isn't this the secret of the wide dispersal of food plants in the Pacific? Was there not in every generation a man, or many men, who had starved for months, and ever celebrated the miracle of salvation by conserving food for others?

There was much to think about on the island, but we

122

thought of little but whales. Sometimes we lay behind the reef all night, sometimes we ran for the shelter of the Tau reef, once or twice we camped ashore on one of the *motus*. At the end of the week we returned, without having seen a whale, and I was nearly sick with disappointment.

But the girls massaged me, and the musicians came; a choir from the palace sang sweet songs, we made kava, and Manutuli, the three-hundred-pound fiddler in the string band, mimed and clowned us to a state of bubbling laughter. The girls put on costumes, oiled and shining like themselves, costumes of shells or parrot feathers or shining folded pandanus, with feather and shell bangles and anklets and coronets, and danced the ancient love stories in their *tau'olungas*.

Tokilupe danced superbly, a strange bright light in her large and lovely eyes, and when she came to the end she sat down beside me.

"By this time Senituli's baby will be born," she said, and I was amazed.

"Why do you think so?"

"It was starting to come while I was changing my costume. It must be here by now, I think." She was quite composed.

"And you just left your own sister to have her baby while you came and danced?" I marvelled.

Stella, on my other side, had the answer to that one.

"Every girl must paddle her own canoe, Olefi," she reminded me.

Senituli's baby was a fine big boy and he was named after me, Olaf Ruhen Latu. But the mother and the aunts and grandmother carried the compliment a step further; they broke the law by refraining to register the birth for nineteen days so that the lad, officially at least, would have the same birthday as myself. It was a considered compliment of which I am very proud.

9

THE third week of whaling opened with the same dull and driving weather, making life difficult in the open boats. Usually I slept at night in the launch under shelter; sometimes when the weather was wild all the men slept there, and there was no room for them to lie down. They slept night after night seated in two rows facing each other, their backs against the cabin walls, their feet intermingled in the passageway, damp and crowded and waiting for the dawn.

Sometimes we slept on Tanieli's island. Tanieli was another whaler who had, in addition, a coconut plantation on one of the *motus*. Here we were welcome guests. Tanieli had come into the whaling business in 1954 when he harpooned a whale from a canoe he operated singlehanded, just as Johnny Siola'a had done. Tanieli's harpoon was fixed to a line carried in a drum in another canoe paddled by an employee. In 1955 he repeated the performance and made enough money to build his own boat in 1956. Whaling in it, he was caught by a victim's flipper and thrown high in the air, landing unhurt forty yards from the vessel. From that moment he was a confirmed whaler, one of the best.

From this island we ranged north and east, far out across the recognized laneways, but we saw no whales. We were beginning to fear that the season would show none, and we found other factors that the weather to blame.

Around the New Zealand coast, two months before, a Russian fleet had straddled the columns of migrating humpbacks and had taken 1399 of them, one less than the "quota" which, set by an international body for the annual slaughter of whales, seems nothing more than a heartless dissimulation based only upon the capacity of the motherships to process the meat. Aided by searching helicopters, furnished with all modern equipment, modern chasers can make heavy inroads on whale populations; the whale, once sighted, has no chance of survival except in the delay caused by the slaughter of his fellows.

These Russian kills were made from the same stream as wintered in Tonga, and it was not only the direct reduction in numbers that endangered our chances. For every whale taken is killed at a time when it is in the company of others, and its death may be counted on to leave its companions apprehensive and nervous.

In the two years, 1963 and 1964, in which the Russian fleet operated on this channel of the humpback migration, they put out of business the New Zealand bay whaling operation of the Tory Channel Whaling Company, better known as the Perano Brothers. This had held through ninety years and four generations of the family, and had in fact perpetuated the early whaling operations in New Zealand.

But the Peranos had developed the hunt in a manner unique in the world; from 1916 they used fast V-bottom chasers which could speed at from twenty-five to thirty knots in the open ocean, though they were small in size, with wooden hulls, and were crewed by one or two men only. A pair of these would round up the

125

whales as dogs herd sheep, and with explosive guns and explosive harpoons they showed excellent results with few men. At one stage they used electric harpoons; they were not slow to seize on innovations. They never endangered or diverted the whale migrations; but the huge operations of the northern hemisphere, spreading north of the Antarctic, destroyed so much of the world's whale stock that 1964 was the last year for the Peranos.

We had premonitions of these disasters as we cruised the *Velata* along the empty sea lanes in that same year and watched the Cooks, Johnny Siola'a, Tanieli Uhila, and occasionally others, fruitlessly searching the horizons. If we could be there first, the weather again and again sent us to our eyrie on Malinoa.

The southern beach, open to the worst of the wind, had suddenly sprouted two dead trees from the branches of which white tatters of flesh hung in clumps, forty or fifty clumps, waving wildly. Old Vai, the *makafeke* fisherman, was catching octopus and drying them for sale and storage.

I went round to see him where he had made a tight little camp, intended to last a month or more, with a few coconut fronds. With a small fire burning he was very warm and comfortable, and he was living on his catch; but he was happy to accept a present of a few tapioca roots. *Makafeke* fishing is such a wonder and a marvel that I almost forgot the empty whaling routes while I listened to old Vai telling me the story and the song. It is a pretty song, about the kingfisher, Sikota, whose name has cadences like those of the English phrase, "There you are", with the last syllable heavily accented.

> *Sikota, Sikota; Kuma, Kuma,*
> *Koe fe a lulu mo Sikota?*
> *Nau O'o ta hotau vaka*
> *Ta he langi tu'o fiha?*

> *Ta he langi tu'o ua*
> *Tuai mai pe vave mai?*
> *To e la'a faifai mai.*

An approximate translation runs:

> *Rat, Rat, let me know*
> *Where did the Owl and the Kingfisher go?*
> *Have you seen them going by?*
> *They're working in the Second Sky.*
> *Will they come home soon or late?*
> *Till the sun sets they will wait. . . .*

Sikota, the kingfisher, had enlisted the help of the Owl, for he was building a canoe to take all the birds for a voyage, a wonderful, exciting voyage. They built the canoe with great care, and they were all ready to set sail when the Crab asked if he could come. The happy birds said "Welcome", and the Rat, too, decided to come along.

All went well for the first part of the voyage, but Crab and Rat soon made themselves unpopular. They were not good sailing companions, for while the birds enjoyed the picnic these two were stealing the food. When the birds saw them and objected, they could do nothing, for Crab and Rat scuttled away under the gratings of the canoe into some dark hole where the birds could not follow. In fact, they took up residence there and stole food that could not be protected from them, and were so anti-social and unco-operative that Sikota decided to teach them a lesson. With his big strong beak he picked and picked at the bottom of the canoe until it began to sink; and when that happened all the birds simply took flight and went home.

And Crab, too, was all right. He didn't listen to the lamentations of Rat; he simply left the hole in the bottom of the canoe and went down to the bottom of the sea where he was quite at home. In vain Rat asked him to consider their fellowship; Crab showed quite clearly he had been interested in nothing but the stolen food. So there was Rat, clinging to the wreckage, out on the wide ocean, and far from home.

But along came Feke, the octopus, and Rat called him. The octopus, a friendly fellow, was concerned by Rat's condition and his threatening fate. He readily agreed to take him to land. Rat sat on his head, and Feke swam for home, very seriously and conscientiously. Rat's spirits lifted, but he couldn't be kind to anyone, he couldn't be thankful; when he saw that he was near the land and certain to get there he lifted his tail and emptied his bowels on Feke's head. Feke, swimming strongly for the shore with his passenger, didn't notice. But when they reached the beach and Rat scampered high up to the safety of dry land, he turned to Feke and said, "Well, thank you for the ride. I've left you a little something in return. Just feel on the top of your head."

Feke felt there, and when he found what Rat had left he was furious. But the more he was angry, the more he protested, the more Rat laughed. And since that day every octopus has hated every rat.

And what has this to do with Vai? The *makafeke* with which he caught his octopus was the representation of a rat. First of all, a heavy stone had been carved and ground into a cone, and lashed to a short curved stick which might have represented the tail of a rat. Cross-sticks represented the legs, and were adorned with tassels. On the back was lashed a carapace consisting of two carved interlocking shells of the chocolate cowrie; and the whole thing, the *makafeke*, was suspended from a string looped at the top end to take the hand.

The fisherman dropped the *makafeke* into the water and jiggled it so that it performed a rat dance a few

128

feet above the shallow bottom. Any octopus whose attention was drawn to this strange matter immediately flew into a paroxysm of rage and launched itself at the supposed rat, changing its own colour through a palette of angry colours, red and brown and yellow. At this moment the fisherman lifted the *makafeke* above the surface, swiftly, for the octopus would tear the construction to pieces otherwise, and reached down his other hand to take the devilfish, swiftly, neatly, efficiently.

If two octopuses see the *makafeke* at the same time the smaller will abandon the brief chase in favour of the larger, but will return when the larger one has been caught.

As if these matters were not enough, Vai and every other Tongan *makafeke* man has two simulated rats, one for high tide, the other for low. Certainly at high tide the suspending string has to be longer, but this is not an essential difference. That lies in the colour, for the chocolate cowrie varies in colour more than any other of the cowrie species, and the specimens that provide their shells for the *makafeke* have to be very carefully chosen. A high tide *makafeke* will arouse no interest in octopuses at low tide, and vice versa. But neither one is the colour of a rat. It is very strange, but there is no other effective lure.

Vai stayed on Malinoa six weeks, eating shellfish and octopus and the few coconuts the island provided. He was an old man, and content to rest between tides or in heavy weather. He took home about a hundred octopuses, all dried and packed in baskets, all dead of an insatiable hatred for the insulter of their race.

The octopus does seem to hate the rat. There are islands where octopuses come ashore and lie in wait on the dry reef for rats, which they seem able to attract to their vicinity. In these islands, too, certain devilfish climb the pandanus trees to drop the ripening fruit into the sea. It seems a traveller's tale, but it is not.

Contacts such as this with Vai, and at sea, the brief thrilling glimpses of shark and mako, of turtle and pelagic predators, could always fascinate my interest for a time, but my quest was for whale, and we had been at sea three weeks before we saw a whale of any sort. This first specimen was a humpback calf, twenty to twenty-five feet in length—which, in the vital statistics of the cetacean, delimits a baby much too young to leave its mother.

In writing of whales it is easy to be guilty of the pathetic fallacy; their reactions seem considered and logical, they seem to answer stimuli as humans do, and it is normal for us to associate with such reactions the same kind of emotions as those with which we ourselves are familiar.

My experience of porpoises, though much too brief for my satisfaction, has made me aware that porpoises sometimes think in much the same way as humans. They have a similar sense of rough humour: a porpoise with a ball poised on his snout, given the target choice of an unsuspecting man with his back turned or a co-operative one with his arms outstretched, will throw it at the first man nearly every time. A porpoise is always tender with human babies, will form strong attachments to individuals—not necessarily those who feed him— and loves the friendly sound of voices.

There seems no clue in prehistory as to why animals of the whale kind should have developed an intelligence or a sensory system with points of contact for that of humans. The original land animal that entered the sea to become the ancestor of the whale was, the scientists tell us, an anteater, or something of the sort; the baleen whales still confine their eating to the marine equivalent of insects. The more intelligent elephant family, or that branch which, undoubtedly after a period of the

130

reflection of which elephants are capable, turned to a maritime existence, begot the dugong and the manatee; neither of these, insofar as my brief knowledge takes me, is capable of evoking the sympathetic understanding the human accords to the whale and the porpoise.

So, though I have regard for the danger of investing whales with the capacity for human emotions, I recognize times when due thought will justify the course, and this was one of them. The little fellow we first observed was panicky and agitated. He kept rising to the surface in unpredictable directions, blowing only once before descending, where other whales would have paused to take three or four or even eight to ten breaths. He seemed to search the depths, and his actions convinced us that his mother had been killed the day before. When we returned to port at week's end we discovered that Tofa Ramsay's crew had put an explosive charge into an accompanied cow on the day we thought, but that a misjudgment or a mischance had sent it to the bottom. But the appearance of this whale in itself was encouraging; and we were in better spirits when we returned to Nuku'alofa for the weekend.

At three o'clock in the morning when we set out on the following Monday there was no wind, and our launch, *Kaimoana*, towed us out to the grounds. With the daylight came a freshening breeze, and we cast loose. Within ten minutes we sighted two humpbacks, a cow with her calf, playing ahead of us. They were running cross-wind, and we began the process of tacking upwind to position ourselves for a downwind run on target. As we did so we raised the sight of a third whale.

At first these sightings had been indications only— the drifting grey and foggy balloons of spouts, or an occasional glimpse of a black fin or section of tail—but presently these indications and their originators became defined more clearly, and the patterns of movement showed us what was going on. Whaling men can tell from the shape of the spouting the breed of whale that caused it, since the cloud is moulded by the shape and position of the nostrils, whether or not they have a common entrance to the body, and by the power of the expulsion from the lungs. The tyro whaler might mistake for a spout the drifting spray from a wave-break on a reef, but with a little experience he would soon learn that, because of differences in temperature and consistency, the two are not at all alike.

On this occasion the third whale was a bull trying to engage the attention of the cow that had the calf—a premature move on his part, for though the humpback leaves the Antarctic and seeks the wintering grounds of Tonga mainly for breeding purposes and indeed is believed not to eat at all in that season, the mothers accompanied by young seem to keep the males at a considerable distance. This one's baby was not more than fifteen feet in length; it had not long been born and the cow seemed embarrassed by the bull's proximity.

The baby helped us keep track of its mother's whereabouts. It came up to breathe about three times as often as she did, and each time it appeared we could be reasonably sure that its mother was somewhere underneath it. Twenty minutes and more between each breath meant that we would have lost the unaccompanied mother much sooner, though it was not always easy to spot the baby either. It spout was a small one; it seemed less cohesive than the heavy exhalations of the adults, and dispersed quickly in the fresh breeze.

After perhaps an hour the bull seemed to accept that he was not welcome, and headed off. He went upwind, so we stayed with the others. Another reason for our choice lay in David's anxiety to take a whale with her calf so that he could present the calf in its entirety to the Queen—who, in turn, would make generous gifts of the meat to schools and other institutions.

For three hours we had some fancy sailing, with swift and unexpected changes of course, tacking and gybing, heading for any point of the compass at the will of the cow. Twice, when she turned upwind, we called in the launch to tow us, waiting some time because the new crew stood off at too great a distance.

We had replaced the lads who had run off; the new men had sea experience. Fevaliaki was a brother of David's, well used to the sea. His name means "Very overwrought; too faint and weak to do anything"; and certainly he was one of the less efficient of the Fifita brothers, but he could handle a boat. The engineer was Manase Vailea; in an early encounter with a whale the running rope had smashed his leg and he had suffered a great deal of unnecessary pain in order that the whale might be secured. Sifa Pa'angi was a taxi-driver in Bloomfield's employ. He was more or less deputizing for Teiapa'a, who had left us, temporarily he hoped, because his father, ill in hospital, was worried about his going to sea and made him promise to stay home.

But this launch crew had too many keen fishermen. Whenever they stopped they got the lines down, and I had a suspicion, born partly of my increasing disappointment, that they stopped in areas where there were likely to be fish rather than in a strategic relationship to *Velata's* course.

The launch's best speed was about four knots, and this was reduced, though very slightly, when she had *Velata* in tow. Since this approximated the cruising speed that whales like best, the upwind tow was always interminably long. In fact, we banked on the whales stopping somewhere to play; but these two had had their fun earlier in the day, and on the second upwind run we lost them.

In good weather whales use the sunlit hours of winter mornings to play and bask. By two o'clock each afternoon they seem to settle to serious travelling, and then it is hopeless to hunt them under sail or with the sweeps. Night hunting is precluded because of the impossibility, in the best of moonlight, of keeping whales in sight, though their grunting and splashing is sometimes heard for hours together. A night encounter would also, of course, provide unexpected and probably unwelcome excitement; acute perception seems essential.

In the days and weeks that followed, we came close to many whales—close enough, once, to a mother and calf to see the lurking tiger-sharks beneath the adult's great belly. The baby, so my crew told me, was big enough to be safe; the sharks were probably concealing their hunters' bulk from the light backdrop of the ocean's surface with some lesser quarry in mind.

We grew familiar with almost every aspect of the whale: the almost batrachian head, ridged and riven in regular patterns as if sculptured from massy vulcanite, the great adjoining expanse of back that terminates in a small dorsal fin, the variable line where the yellow of the underneath parts meets the black of the upper, the unwinking eye, the crater of the single nostril, the rigid curving mouth. And the predictable forms of movements: the effortless thrust of the stiff forward parts, the seemingly endless roll of the posterior column, lithe and lissom in the dive, the sweep of swim fins, the exquisite poise and balance of the manipulated tail.

I was lost in admiration one morning at the antics of a mother and daughter leaping high in the air—a leap of more than fifty feet for the mother, a prodigious expenditure of energy. This was a large whale, sixty feet long; and the very large calf, approaching forty feet, seemed ready for an independent life. There was an hour or more of advanced calisthenics, demonstrations interrupted by undersea excursions which effectively kept the whales at distances of up to a few hundred yards from us. Then the cow seemed to stand on her head in the sea so that her fluked tail, a thing of beauty, was raised upon the slim and shapely pedestal of her nether end and stood twenty to twenty-five feet in the air.

"This peaking of the whale's flukes," wrote Herman Melville, "is perhaps the grandest sight to be seen in all animated nature. Out of the bottomless profundities the gigantic tail seems spasmodically snatching at the highest heaven."

There was nothing spasmodic about the gesture we now saw; indeed it testified to great control and deliberation. Melville wrote of the peaking of flukes as a preliminary to sounding, and he wrote of the sperm rather than the humpback. The humpback at large seems a more active whale than the sperm and, possessing as it does a greater immensity of bulk in proportion to its length than any other whale, is furnished with enormous fins and a magnificent tail, more shapely to my eye than any other. No wonder that over the ages seamen found the epitome of beauty in the matching of the whale's tail with the woman's body; there ought to be mermaids for the sheer beauty of the concept.

The whale that we marked this August morning stayed on her head in one place like a devotee of yoga, and very slowly, very deliberately, lowered the great flag of her flukes upon its flexible standard to caress the surface of the sea with a sweeping motion. The gesture occupied about twenty seconds and, with a break between each demonstration during which the column of the tail stood vertical, was repeated fourteen times.

I said, "I wonder what on earth that means."

Sioeli Kaho said, "It means 'Good-bye Olefi'."

So it proved, though we didn't think so at the time, and continued with the chase.

In their earlier acrobatics these two had given me the most breath-taking vision I had ever had of the whale in its world. In perfect formation they came rushing up through the furrowed sea only fifty or sixty yards away, up, up into the air until they stood as high as a five-storey building, up, up, and up; then at the top of the leap each leaned slightly to port and fell, the two great bodies within a few yards of each other, the wide ribbed fins visibly showing the fingers like the bones in the wings of bats, until they were tucked tidily to the figured black-and-yellow flanks for the smack of re-entry, as loud as cannon, fountaining the ocean to the clouds in an amazing mass that made a white and glittering solid of the sunlight it enclosed.

We were constantly being entertained in this way by the attitudes, or what might better be described as the gestures, of whales. Though they obviously have a limited repertoire, they seem enthusiastic in presenting its whole range. Beneath the surface where they spend most of their lives (often coming up to breathe less than three times in an hour) their acrobatics must be wonderful indeed. This impression seems confirmed by the way whales seek out the ocean shallows. Humpbacks seem inclined to take any opportunity of visiting places where the bottom lies at twenty fathoms or less —even though their protection from natural marine enemies is said to lie in their ability to dive deeper.

William Dampier, the pirate who invented and established the important modern science of oceanography, made a similar note in the course of a voyage to Australia in 1699. On 18th August of that year he wrote:

> We had an abundance of whales about the ship, some ahead, others astern and some on each side making a very dismal noise but when we came out again into deeper water they left us. Indeed the noise they made by blowing and dashing of the sea with their tails, making it all of a breach and foam was

dreadful to us, like the breach of the waves in very shoal water or among rocks. The shoal these whales were on had a depth of water sufficient, no less than twenty fathoms as I said, and it lies in latitude 22 degrees 22 minutes.

This was a latitude equivalent to that of Tonga, and these were the humpbacks that annually, in the season centring on August, drive northwards along the West Australian coast. Since the whales do not feed at this season the attraction of the shoal could, I think, be the opportunity it affords them of enjoying, as they very obviously do, their athletic prowess, in evolutions impossible at the surface. It must be like the attraction a cumulus cloud exerts on an airman, a challenge and a joy.

Again and again that week there were moments when all hands brightened to the cry of "Tofua'a", meaning "whale", or more frequently "Puna", the sea-dividing "leap". Again and again we set out in chase, without success. We came near, but never near enough to cast an iron, and the only grim satisfaction we could glean was that no other boat was successful either. It was a lean solace; we would have liked to have seen a success for any one of the half-dozen boats at Tonga-tapu; but their continued failure seemed assurance that our own was not due to incompetence.

At Ha'apai, in the north, there was rather more success. The first capture there had been made within three-quarters of an hour of the licence being issued; it was taken with explosive. Some of our lads had been a little envious; it seemed such a simple way to take a whale. Now we heard another side of that method.

A Ha'apai whaler, seeing a whale basking on the surface, drove up on him, setting the whaler high and dry on his back. This was what we all hoped to do; it confirmed the best advantage we could secure; it gave

137

opportunity for a careful placement of the harpoon. This time, with gelignite attached to the iron, the headsman chose his target carefully and drove the iron deep below the blubber into the strata of muscle beneath, a classic dart. On this the whale should have dived for the depths, leaving the whaler afloat on the surface, waiting for the explosion. Instead he lay supine, perhaps no more troubled by the bite of an iron than a man with a flea; perhaps trying to estimate the forces arranged against him. He didn't move a muscle, but the spark slid down the fuse towards the detonator, while the headsman watched it horrified. He had no means of dealing with this. He was too hard aground to push off. He thought of reaching for the lance, to prod the whale into movement, but it was not immediately at hand, and he had no result from pushing again on the handle of the harpoon.

When detonation was near he leapt for the stern of the whaler, with all his crew. The explosion when it came blew the bows of the boat to pieces. The men had a five-mile swim for the shore. They all reached it safely, with their means of livelihood reduced to a few splinters far out on the sea. Presumably the whale was killed and sank; no trace of it remained.

10

WE made the weekend a long one; repairs and replacements kept us busy, but the main delay was in arranging finance to buy oil for the diesel and food for the men. The Pan-Pacific and South-East-Asian Conference of Women's Organizations had come to Nuku'alofa, and the little town had been groomed and sweetened, lawns cut and swept, roads cleared of market stalls, houses painted by official request. Above the bread shop the storekeeper set out all his treasures: carvings of the Royal Dove, the Royal Lion, President Kennedy, and several other subjects; in the window of the boxing stadium a display of watercolour paintings testified to a remarkable ineptitude.

These had nothing to do with the official displays of handiwork, which were breath-taking: weaving nine hundred years old and finer than linen, and all kinds of artifacts so beautifully made that one could not recapture in imagination the patience and skill that went to their making.

In the evening there was a concert on the Government *mala'e,* where an impressive stage had been erected and decked with fronds and flowers, and here a play written by Her Majesty Queen Salote was the central attraction. She had written the words and music; it was less a play than a word-and-action tribute to the passing year, each month making its contribution in turn. The Queen, who is a composer of no mean ability, had incorporated a great deal of the traditional significance of the passing months, and I was trying with some difficulty to follow when an interruption came in the shape of six shipwrecked sailors.

These were the very well-preserved survivors of the Californian ketch *Diablo*. She had made a fast passage from Hawaii to Tahiti and was working back westerly across the Pacific to Fiji when she hit the reef between the islands of Tau and One. She had gone up in the bright clear starlight of the calmest night we had seen in a month, at four o'clock in the morning, in full view of two lighthouses, and apparently without reference to the echometer or any other item of the modern gear that was provided in the interests of safe navigation. Within two hours of striking the reef, on which she had driven high and hard, though both the break and the islands were visible at a distance of a mile in those conditions, her crew had been rescued by Johnny Siola'a on the first leg of his whaling sweep. He had also removed all her more valuable equipment; in fact the owner, when I first heard him, was telling all and sundry that they could help themselves to what remained.

It must have been a strange day for them all; beginning with shipwreck and moving through rescue and salvage to the *mala'e* where, in pantomime, Fu'ufu'unekinanga, the Month of Abundant Life, as the August-September moon is called, was vacating centre-stage— as in real life it was vacating the sky—in favour of 'O'oa'fangongo, the Basket-and-Funnel that symbolizes the scanty crops of the September-October moon when men in the fields prepare for seeding time.

"I am a sudden shiver of beauty," sang Abundant

Life, dressed in the flaring colours of plenty, posturing mid-stage with fruits and flowers in a profusion few theatres can afford:

> *I am a sudden shiver of beauty,*
> *Cool breezes restless with the song's delirium,*
> *Green valleys raptured by new leaves,*
> *Young yams in leaf, and man enclosed*
> *In summer happiness and peace.*

The dancing, I thought, was slightly inferior to what we enjoyed night after night in the intimacy of our house, but it was still active in the eye of my mind when we sailed only a few hours later. We had lost our tough and voluble Olive, for he was a member of the Royal Guard, which was much in demand in this week of conference. And Ve'etutu's active life was playing up with him; he was walking too many miles too often to see his girlfriend whenever he could come ashore; this weekend he was ill and tired and missed the boat. David took over as sailing-master.

But eleven-year-old Fifita was on school holidays. He had been promised a week or two of whaling, as in other parts a schoolboy may be promised a week or two of riding after cattle. The difference was that he could be given no quiet horse; he took the same risks as the men, he was under the same obligation to look out for himself, and to move like a leaping fish to do so. He would be useful in the boat; strength is handy but far from essential at sea. Accompanying him were Hopoate and Sonny Vincent the Papalangi again.

We thought we were in luck from the beginning. We had hardly sailed past Malinoa Island when we raised a cow whale and her calf. Our first two passes missed, but we had not frightened the animals. The two Cook boats were operating not far away and they came in immediately to the centre of the excitement. Ned Cook yelled out to David: "If she comes my way I'm coming in."

David agreed, which surprised me, for I thought that like me he would have already established a proprietary right; but he thought it fair enough for each of us to take our turn. Before long the Cooks were committed. It was a delight to see the way the two little sloops quartered the sea and started in lively pursuit, one on the port tack, one on the starboard. But it soon became apparent that they did not want to press home the engagement while we stood by. The skippers were under the mistaken impression that the gelignite they had prepared for their harpoons was illegal; probably they did not altogether trust the presence of non-Tongans in Roger and myself, and wished us gone before they used it. They were manoeuvring, therefore, to get the whale on the run rather than corner it; they counted on having sufficient speed to overtake it when they got it travelling. This tactic would have been at best a dubious ploy for us. *Velata* was slower into the wind, and did not have the advantage of a companion in pursuit.

As soon as he recognized this reluctance on their part, David made a run in after the whale, setting right across the bows of the Cook boat then in position. She and her companion drew away at that and left the quarry to us.

She was huge, an enormous whale, the biggest humpback, I think, that I have ever seen anywhere, with a small calf, less than twenty feet. I estimated the calf's length myself at fifteen, but David thought it more. It had been born some time, for its back had acquired a coat of black, replacing the creamy white of its birth colour. The pair reminded me of early years when I had shepherded the high country in New Zealand: frequently the largest, fattest ewe would drop a midget lamb.

We pursued this whale with even more determination than we had previously brought to the chase. Several times during the day we thought we were working down on her at exactly the right time. But again and again, moving so slowly that her disappearance was agonizing, she went down just before we arrived. We could see her great black bulk beneath us as we sailed over, and again we saw the *tenifa,* the tigersharks that lurk beneath the belly of a nursing whale, attracted, so the Tongans say, by the milk that escapes from the mighty stream tapped by the calf, or by the smell of milk, which is expelled by the mother rather more than it is extracted by the baby. The new-born calf is vulnerable to the *tenifa,* but in a few days is safe.

After five and a half hours committed to this chase we made our last and most nearly successful pass. We were driving down a dying wind, directly at her port fin, more slowly than we would have liked, but still at about five knots, and we were almost on her. I had been under the impression that she was watching our arrival; several times before we must have been clearly visible to her over her head as she sank, but this time we must have taken her unawares. We were no more than thirty feet away when she gave a convulsive and very violent shudder, and sank very quickly.

We had eight yards of nylon rope between the harpoon and the sisal, so that our limit was a cast of twenty-four feet; and this was further reduced by the distance the iron had to sink in the blubber and the angle at which it struck. To be thirty feet from a rabbit is a big miss; but thirty feet from a seventy-foot whale is a narrow margin; and this final disappointment ended our day.

If our day had its frustrations, young Fifita's must have been worse. His eagerness was reflected in his handsome bright lively boyish face; he lived for the moment when he could come to grips with the whale, and when we were committed to the chase he fondled a

143

little knife; for he had promised Madeleine that he would put her name on the first whale we caught; he would cut it into the hide and it would be hers.

But when we came really close Maile or Tevita—not his father—would tell him to take cover, to climb under the helmsman's deck, and he would do so without a murmur though the position precluded him from seeing anything of the excitement. I marvelled at this self-discipline; it was from some such quality in their youngsters that the Polynesians developed the amazing potential by which they covered the hemisphere in tiny vessels.

We ran for an island shelter for the night, and passed close to *Diablo* on the Tau reef, a tragic sight. She was surrounded by a small flotilla of boats salvaging equipment in spite of the wild seas on the knives of coral. Roger Bath wanted to take photographs of the wreck, but the light was poor; we thought it best to come back in the morning.

It was a lucky enough decision; in the wild wind of morning we could not have chased whale, but behind the Tau reef there was a fair enough shelter. The tide would not let us approach the wreck, but one or two lighter boats had stayed overnight, in pools among the coral. We laid off, and some of our lads waded and swam to the wreck. They had a quarter of a mile or more of antler coral to negotiate, and I will never understand how, even with the greatest of care, a Tongan can make this way through such a forest of knives without getting seriously hurt. Some six or seven lads went, including little Fifita.

What fantasies possessed him? What delirious delights and satisfactions did he know as he explored the wreck, packed with a romantic cargo from exotic ports like San Francisco and Los Angeles? He would be a hero of sorts when he returned to school. Meantime there was the joy of scrambling through the wreck,

144

awash in heavy seas on the cruel rock, the bottom torn quite away from her.

Some of the wreckers had been chipping away at the masts, and now we saw them fall. Our lads, quite properly, took command of them, and took, too, all the standing and running gear with which they had been furnished. They belonged now, not to the overgenerous owner, but to the insurance company. After a while, as the tide rose, they swam the masts out to us; five lads with the mainmast, Lau'ia swimming alone with the mizzen on which, riding astride, came young Fifita, clutching a box filled with minor salvage: a torch, a set of wood-carving chisels, a sheath-knife, a pot of caviar and one of smoked crab, a table-knife and a screw-driver. We took the masts in tow and landed them safely on the island of Ata, dragging them high above the tide.

It was near evening then, and Roger and I decided to make our meal ashore. The wind was coming out of the north as we rode the whale-boat in, and above us was a cloud, very dark, split with a peculiar bright white gulf, as though it had been cut with a knife. Just as we neared the shore the wind, from blowing in our faces, switched to our backs, a hundred-and-eighty-degree change in the fastest time I have ever experienced, blasting in violently, carrying a wild content of rain.

We jumped for the beach and ran, and finally found shelter under a section of corrugated-iron roofing the only function of which was to collect rainwater and feed it into the island tank. It was a little sheltered from the wind, and we made toast and toasted cheese: I grilled a bonito we had caught an hour before and Roger heated canned hamburger and onions, attracting the attention of a skinny cat that seemed not at all interested in my ample supply of good fish. There were chickens everywhere, hens with clutches of six- or eight-day-old youngsters. And obviously there was no trouble here with rats or snakes.

Next day, from the first glimmering of light, we headed west, and three hours from the island we sighted two whales, a mother and her calf, again good big ones. They announced their presence first with a long high beckoning fin, lifted straight up towards the grey sky, with the tip turned towards us, exactly as if the whale was beckoning. Then both whales started jumping. We had a chase that lasted the rest of the day, but the pair never gave us a chance. They would work around in an encouraging sort of way and then, after a long submersion, show upwind of us again. We would call in *Kaimoana*, and the long tow would begin. When we were free of the tow and the whales were to our lee the joy would start.

These two were brilliantly beautiful; and leapt so high and so deliberately that we couldn't help but wonder what in their element propelled them into the air with so little apparent impetus. The splash that creamed the water when they fell back must have been three hundred feet across; the sound of the belly-slap, even in that rough weather, carried clearly over more than half a mile.

We returned to a quieter weekend. I had an open coral sore on my leg which, in the constant wash of saltwater, refused to heal. Madeleine's leg had been deeply ripped by a dog, and both of us were attending hospital when we could.

We returned the *Diablo's* masts and gear to the insurance company's representative, and were somewhat mortified to learn that the owner had given an interview to the American press in which he commented on the thieving propensities of Tongans! By that time he was probably feeling a little sick over the unnecessary loss of his ship, but the wild accusations, no more than lightly justified, came strangely from a rich man for

146

whom the poor were doing so much without thought or hope or reward.

Fifita put on his best clothes, gathered up his little box of salvage, and took it to the owner, who, in a generous moment, presented him with what it contained.

I was interested, this weekend, to leaf through David's reading. It included: Nicholl's *Concise Guide to the Navigation Examinations,* North's *Nautical Tables,* Ageton's *Dead Reckoning Altitude and Azimuth Tables* (U.S. Navy, Third Edition), Brown's *Signalling,* and the *New Method English Dictionary* (written specially for the foreigner).

In this weekend, too, I took note of a rather remarkable demonstration of Tongan ingenuity. There was an arrangement by which the radio station would incorporate in its programme messages for the smaller islands to which there was no other means of communication. For larger islands, of course, normal channels had to be used, though naturally these were not as efficient as the station and, for public messages, did not command so large a distribution. I wasn't surprised, therefore, to hear a message from the Inspector of Police to the small island of Eueiki that the island trading ship *Ulufonoa* would call next day and the population should get everything ready for her so that there would be no delays. There was only one thing wrong with this message: the *Ulufonoa* never called at Eueiki, and there was no intention of sending her. She was instead going to the large island of Eua; but Government regulations forbade the sending of this message to Eua, which was well populated and well serviced with more regular communications. The Inspector of Police knew that everyone knew the score, that they would make the deduction, obvious to a Tongan, that *Ulufonua* was about to make her call at Eua where the people would get ready, while the Eueiki people took no notice.

Under some pressure from the youngsters David agreed to go out for the day only on Monday; it was my birthday, and they wanted to celebrate. But the weather on Monday was too bad anyway, though brave talk had half-convinced the crew that they'd bring in a whale as a present to me. At night the celebration was confined to our own house, and we could have no music, for one of the Tongan nobles had just died. Under normal circumstances there could be no music of any kind on the island for at least five days; but once again the intrusions of the outside world played havoc with tradition. The Pan-Pacific Congress of Women's Organizations was still meeting; it was a pet project of Queen Salote's and the programme, drawn up weeks before, had shown a concert for this night. The concert went on as planned, the Tongans who attended wearing mourning.

The next day the weather continued too bad to go to sea. The centre-board had been jamming in its box, and we slipped it away to the harbour bottom and brought it ashore. With Tongan ingenuity it had been cut from a heavy steel pipe such as is used for oil lines or electric power poles. It had been slit down one side and straightened out, and had tended to reassume the original curve. We brought it up to the smithy and straightened it and, when it was right, put it back, sliding it up into place from underneath. The swimming and diving ability of the crew saved us several times from the necessity of slipping one or other of the boats.

About this time we saw a movie that purported to show Hawaii in pre-European days. It carried a preamble promising that everything in the picture was authentic—customs, dances, religious ceremonies—a promise backed by certain institutions of learning. The first scene in the picture showed Hawaiians swimming out in a great crowd to a visiting ship; all were using the overarm stroke which was not introduced to the

148

world until the beginning of the twentieth century. So much for the standards of established scholarship. Nearly all unsophisticated Polynesians swim with arms beneath the water, in a quiet controlled stroke that does not attract sharks. The whole body is often beneath the surface. And at underwater work there are few experts to beat the islanders.

While we worked on the centre-board David said, "I think it would be very nice, Olefi, if you were to stay with us longer than you plan, say till the first week in October. This would mean you are in Tonga for as long as we were on Minerva Reef. The boys think this would be appropriate."

I protested that my stay in Tonga was a delightful interlude, not to be compared at all to the ordeal they had faced on their reef. But since October would take us past the end of the whaling season I agreed to stay.

David had, of course, an additional reason for his suggestion. A cruise ship, the *Kuala Lumpur*, was in port and it was proposed to take her to the northern ports of Vava'u and Ha'apai—the first time any tourist ship had visited all these places. David was needed as pilot. He was away some days, during which he conned his big charge through the channels and made and left each port in the dark.

Now David's place as whaling-master was taken by Tevita Uaisele. I awoke some time after two in the morning and went down to the harbour. There was no wind at all, and we towed *Velata* to sea with *Kaimoana*. About eight-thirty a good breeze sprang up, but the crew showed no inclination to cast off and go looking for whale. They had a drum of sweet potatoes cooking on an open fire on *Kaimoana's* deck.

The weather was dull, dark, and misty; we had lost the lights of Nuku'alofa only about two miles from the shore, and there was no lessening of this effect with the rising wind. When the sweet potatoes were cooked and

149

distributed we parted company and, in spite of the driving drizzle, within ten minutes raised the sight of two whales, a mother and a baby, playing ahead of us. We were running across the wind, and they were a little upwind of our course, so we began the process of tacking to get upwind of them and to keep in a good position for a downwind run.

Soon we raised the sight of a third whale, just glimpses of his spout at first, then movements of fin or tail, and finally an identification of a bull, prematurely interested in the mother with the baby. The light became better, and occasionally the sun momentarily broke through the clouds. We chased the pair for hours, tacking and gybing, taking every advantage of the wind; and the sailing was superb.

Only about twice in this time the whales showed themselves upwind after a long submersion, and each time a short tow with the launch remedied our positional play. Then came a moment when we were running crosswind, searching for the vanished pair which, we feared, were upwind to starboard, when Lau'ia saw fresh balloons of grey spoutings directly downwind. We had then been on the chase for something more than five hours. The new quarry were, perhaps, three quarters of a mile away, but they were static.

Tevita Uaisele, almost perfect in the part of a captain, now spoke to the boys, a piece of oratory that would have meant nothing to me at all, except for the effect it produced. They listened intently to him; his choice of words impressed them as much as his attitude.

All right, boys, he was saying, there's a whale there waiting for us. We're going to run up on him immediately and there'll be a certain amount of commotion; the boat might get thrown around, certainly something unexpected will happen. But every man should do his own job without being too impressed by the whale we're going to catch; he shouldn't worry about the size or the strength; it was just another fish, and, working together, they'd handle it with ease.

When he stopped talking a hush came over the boat; we had experienced this once or twice before when we were close to an engagement; but this time there was an intensity of silence that accented the chuckling of the water at the bow and forward of the rudder. The sound of wind and of water was all.

Maile stripped off his coat and set it in the jaws of the boom where it worked against the mast; no whisper escaped. Solomone and Fine Feuiaki stood to the ballast bags stacked on the lower deck aft around the line-tub. Roger Bath stood up in the port shrouds, balancing on the gunwale, three cameras slung round his neck; Tevita looked worried and motioned him down, but Roger, claiming the prerogative of photographers to be answerable to no one present, took no notice and stayed where he was. Tevita checked the axes in place. Lau'ia saw to the lances and then came aft to take a couple of turns of the whaleline round the loggerhead.

Tevita jumped back up on the harpoon platform, hefting his favourite iron, hafted with a shaft he had carried for many years, a shaft that had brought him most of his whales. Maile Siakumi stood beside him, in a like manner balancing the harpoon that was attached to the sea-anchor with a length of modern polypropaline line.

Both whales were in a perfect position. That is to say, they were downwind of us, cruising downwind themselves and playing a little on the surface, wrapped in each other's company and oblivious of the world. We committed *Velata* to the tail of the nearest, but Tevita seemed undecided which whale to take, signalling Ve'etutu his changes of mind, and three times moving his harpoon and line around the forestay for a port or a starboard attack.

151

Finau moved up on the high deck where Ve'etutu, standing, could steady himself with a hand on his head, and I stood a little ahead of them on the lower deck, just abaft the line-tub.

As we came close to the whale she rolled on her back, exposing her cream-white belly to the sun. Where the cream met the rubber-black skin of the back there was an area where all was flecked, like a map of close-laid islands, like a sky of fractured clouds. The white undersurface of the tail was ringed with a hand-wide band of black.

Ve'etutu had brought us up with a series of slight corrections, directly at the tail. Now, as we almost collided, he turned slightly starboard and then corrected again, bringing us parallel and about nine or ten feet from the flank.

The great yellow belly seemed to spread over yards of ocean; it seemed big enough for a game of tennis. I could not imagine where the fin might lie. At this moment both Maile and Tevita lofted their harpoons and launched them, sinking them truly into the whale. The heads entered the skin with a tiny audible "plop", a sound of which the very insignificance was awesome, signalling as it did the culmination of months of effort. The heads hit simultaneously and two or three feet apart, into the area of variegated skin at the underflank, only eight to ten feet behind the fin.

That "plop" was the last identifiable sound I heard for some time. In the next fraction of a second Maile and Tevita jumped away, one to drop the sail, the other to launch the sea-anchor; then there was pandemonium. I began to turn away from the whale as it whipped right-side-up, like a cat. Its starboard flipper stood against the sky, its tip twenty-five feet high and almost overhead, a thick column that dwarfed our slender mast. It had to come down; it was moving like a falling

152

tree and I could not see how it could miss us; it was more than fifteen feet in length and was upraised additionally above the surface by the convulsing bulk of the great body. The tail was rising. I turned away, whether in fear or instinctive reaction I could not tell. The next moment I was thrown into the boom by the shock of a wall of water hitting *Velata's* beam.

Ve'etutu put the tiller hard over to swing to starboard. Tevita, clearing away the enormous sea-anchor attached to Maile's harpoon, missed his footing while momentarily he decided to help Maile with the throat halyards of the mainsail, Maile having struck trouble. It was an error of judgment for Tevita, and it cost him dear.

The whale was away, and with the action pulled the iron of the sea-anchor against the bows, trapping Tevita by the leg. Maile abandoned the sail and came to his assistance, but already the violence of the strain had skinned Tevita's leg and the deck was slippery with his blood. Next moment the polypropaline line between harpoon and sea-anchor broke—though it was reputed to have a ten-ton breaking strain—and Tevita was free. The mainsail came down with a jerk, and *Velata's* crazed movements ripped the canvas against one of the rowlocks.

I saw this momentarily, in a glimpse only. The jerk that sent me into the main boom and the wall of water accompanying it had, meantime, filled Roger's cameras where he stood on the rail, clutching at the shrouds to save himself. It had also thrown Fine Feuiaki from where he had been bending to dump the ballast, propelling him high into the air towards the stern. He flew like a clay pigeon, over Ve'etutu's head, though Ve'etutu was standing rail high. The two men collided, and the blow knocked Ve'etutu down, but as he went he handed the mainsheet to the flying man, and Fine clung to it, as to his hope of a hereafter.

As the sail came down the mainsheet ran out; there was for a time no resistance, but it had caught over the whale-line and round the loggerhead, running out in the opposite direction to that taken by the whale-line, the wet sheet running astern, the bone-dry brand-new whale-line running forward through the press of tumbled men. The mainsheet was the first wet rope I had ever seen burning with friction; it smoked on the loggerhead, and the smell of hemp afire was harsh in my nose.

I jumped for the loggerhead, recovering from my fall; I jumped and cleared the burning rope and for the first time saw Fine on the other end of it, in the water now, about fifteen feet behind the boat. Lau'ia stood alongside me, cool and ready, clearing the racing whale-line from the tub. Finau, alongside Ve'etutu on the steering platform, was pulling on the mainsheet to bring Fine alongside, and Ve'etutu, in spite of having a difficult job steering at that moment, was trying to help him.

Fine, his arms and head above water, was throwing a bow-wave like a battle cruiser; agony rode his face, and some fear. There was no other help for him at hand; *Kaimoana* should have been standing by, but she was a mile or more astern, and as it turned out was unaware of the man overboard.

I jumped to the steering platform and helped Finau pull Fine close to the boat. I caught him by the right arm and shoulder, and Finau caught him too, and we pulled, but he seemed immovable. On a second attempt I relinquished my own hold of the boat, spread my legs, pushed Finau aside, and gave both my arms and my back to the task, and somehow, but I will never know how, I pulled him aboard. Fine is a big man, weighing 180 pounds, and he came in like a champagne cork from the bottle. He sat gasping, still wearing the expression of agony, until Sioeli called him sharply to come and lay hold on the line which had now slowed to a manageable speed. I jumped forward, and helped Lau'ia dump the ballast and set the mainsheet and boom to one side, safely out of the road.

Velata was dancing, bolting like a colt. The whale had pulled out ninety fathoms of whale-line before she showed the slightest sign of slackening. About thirty fathoms were left in the tubs. Luckily we had hit her over the shallows; and the ninety fathoms appeared to go straight down to the depths, but there should have been no more than forty fathoms of ocean at that point.

Tevita had been quite badly damaged by the whale-line and for a while believed he could not carry on. I believed it, too; his leg was raw and dark and mingled blood and sea-water had stained him everywhere. He came down from the harpoon deck and called on Sioeli and Maile to take charge.

Roger was calling for cloth to dry his cameras. I found a wad of Kleenex in my basket under the after-deck and threw it to him. All his cameras had filled with water in the flurry of the whale, and his pictures, though we were not to know it then, were useless. The open-boat work in bad weather was shockingly hard on his gear; for this and other reasons few of the many hundreds of pictures he took were usable. This was a severe disappointment; the subjects were spectacularly good, and I had depended on his efforts for my own record.

The whale slacked her mighty dive; she had been unprepared for it; her lungs were probably not filled with air. She was returning to the surface, and the crew, headed and encouraged by Sioeli, pulled on the line, bringing *Velata* up on the whale. From forward aft, first Sioeli then William Fa, then Fine, dripping wet and shaking water from him with every exertion, then Solomone Manoa, then Finau, then Lau'ia, all heaving in rhythmic unison, sometimes making a foot or two, sometimes just holding their own against the whale's forward movement.

Now we were committed to what used to be called the Nantucket Sleigh-ride; and I was launched on the forty-five most exciting moments of what has not been altogether a dull life. As soon as the cow surfaced, the bull came from whatever point he had fled to in his first startled moments, and accompanied his love. From the vantage of the steering platform, where I now supported a frantically working Ve'etutu, it was as though we had the two great animals in a double-harness in this lively wonder-ride. The speed was not as great as I had imagined; I guessed it at fourteen or fifteen knots at the start, steadying down to nine or ten. But there were seas to plunge through and swift changes of course, and at base there was an inevitability about the ride, like being hitched to an unpredictable bolting juggernaut, and the excitement did not depend upon the speed factor.

"I tell you, Olefi," Sioeli said later, "when I laid hold on that line it was as if I laid hold on fire; not hot but alive; like fire for the life in it."

The half-dozen men played the part of the reel on a fishing-rod. By their efforts, when the whale changed direction or rose from the deep, we could bring the boat up to her, sometimes as close as twenty-four feet from the harpoon head, at which point the lighter nylon line, designed to break down the heavy work of the harpooner, was joined to a heavy sisal. Since the harpoon head in this instance was located more than this distance ahead of the tail of the quarry, it followed that, when the slack was taken up, the tail overlapped our bows, and every time the whale dived beneath the water, this exquisite potential of destruction (capable of throwing us, boat and all, high in the air, capable of pounding the timber to splinters, the bone and flesh to jelly) seemed to brush the planks. Every time it rose it came down within inches of Maile and Tevita.

The harpoon irons had worked correctly. They were bent back into a fish-hook shape (as they had been designed to do) by the tremendous plunge of the whale; but the wooden handles had not come out of their sockets, and their frenzied vibration under the water-flow contributed to the loosening of the only head holding us. At this stage it would have been possible to have hit the whale with a third, or a third and fourth harpoon. Tevita, however, used the lance.

Six times he seized an opportunity of casting it, and four of these times he drove it deep into the whale, perhaps six feet below the skin. Each time, when he recovered it, there was a delay while he straightened the iron and made the lance usable again. Each time, the whale jumped away beyond the control of the half-dozen men on the line.

The shock of the wound made by the spade-head of the lance, aggravated by the opening action of the round shaft, must have been immense. There was what seemed a considerable loss of blood from three of the wounds; it coloured the ocean; but the reservoir within the mighty veins and arteries was a big one.

As the whale tired she ran increasingly in narrower and narrower circles, frequently doubling back so that, if she were out on a short line at these times, the 32-foot boat spun like a leaf in a whirlpool; it ran some danger of being broached, especially in combination with the plunging of the seas, which were far from calm; the billows and the thrusting whale made high excitement. It made a furious work for Ve'etutu, on the tiller. After a while he shucked his clothes and steered naked, dancing on the platform, laughing and singing, challenging the whale and the seagods, filled with joy. The excitement ran through his hand on my head like an electric current.

The love and faithfulness of the bull, which had survived the swift attack from an element he could not know or understand, did not long survive the increasing agitation and panic of his lover-victim; he headed off in a direction that would take him where we had left the other whales, the mother and her small daughter.

The water below us was so clear that even to a considerable depth we could see details of whale and line. While the contest continued, the wind was dropping. To our joy the whale was heading for Nuku'alofa most of the time—this meant that the subsequent tow would be considerably reduced. A passenger schooner from Ha'apai hove to at a little distance to let her passengers enjoy the spectacle.

Then, after three quarters of an hour, at the fourth successful blow of the lance, the great responsive lunge of the whale ripped away the harpoon and we lost her. The wind continued to drop, there was almost none. If there had been any, our broken sail would have prevented us from taking good advantage of it. We called in the *Kaimoana* and set her to the chase, but though the whale was close to exhaustion and hugged the surface the launch was too slow. We recalled her, and waited for the tow home.

It was then I noticed for the first time the sweat pouring down the faces of the men, faces lit with a nervous excitement. They talked eagerly all the way home, their voices rising and falling, overlapping those of other speakers, a very un-Polynesian procedure, at least among men. Their reaction could not be contained; it was lit with the joy of the chase and hardly dampened at all by the failure. They had seen each man put to the trial, and they were all happy and satisfied. This excitement was not contained until they slept that night. They slept at home, for there were many repairs to be made.

11

So we went on through that season, sometimes alone on the ocean, sometimes in friendly encounter with other whalers. I saw the best ocean sailing of my life on a day when Tofa Ramsay with his big fast power boat *'Alaimoana* came to play interference when we were committed to the chase of a big whale. *'Alaimoana's* intention was to take the whale for herself, but *Velata's* manoeuvrability combined with David's understanding of both sail and whale tactics had us turning inside the power boat each time. After an hour of trying unsuccessfully to come between *Velata* and the whale, *'Alaimoana* turned away.

"I never see such a silly man," Ve'etutu complained. "Does he think this is the only whale in the sea?"

But Tongans rarely start grudge fights. Tofa Ramsay, at the first opportunity, and within the week, tendered apologies and offered handsome amends.

In mid-September the Cook boats caught a small whale with a well-placed charge of explosive. On that day our launch had waited in port to buy oil fuel, and on going to sea had chased another whaler halfway to the Ha'apai group, never closing the gap sufficiently to see more than the top of the sail. We had operated without her, and there were no other power boats in that part of the ocean. Cook's two whalers set their lines on their thirty-ton catch and began to tow it in under sail. Since it was getting towards the end of the whaling day, first Johnny Siola'a and then Tanieli hooked in their boats to the tow. We offered *Velata,* but we were again having trouble with our centre-board and could not have contributed much muscle to the long tow. In a courteous speech shouted over the water, Ned Cook turned down our offer.

For fourteen hours the four whaling boats together hauled on the dead whale; a beautiful sight, and a rare one in these days when sail is used mainly for pleasure: the four little vessels, lashed one behind the other, nodding in unison to the seas that slapped their bows; and the great black bulk rolling behind, its stumpy fin, drilled and roped, like the flag on a buoy rolling in its wake.

Back in port we collected the errant *Kaimoana* and I took her to sea again to act as tug, for there really wasn't enough wind for heavy haulage under sail; but she chose this moment to break down, and we were five hours, more or less, lying a mile or two from shore, trying to get her running again. By that time the silent cortege of whalers was passing Nuku'alofa port, heading for the edge of the reef where the whale would be grounded, and I caught my breath at the beauty of those ghostly sails in the mottled moonlight. I caught my breath and knew that here was a vision my mind would hold for ever.

On the following day, a Saturday when we were not at work, Cook sold out the whale in four hours: the skin, the meat, the blubber, the intestines, and the bones. It was a small whale, thirty-six feet in length and probably not long weaned. It netted £410 Tongan, the Tongan pound having parity with the Australian.

The heart of the whale was not sold. It never is. It is often given to the royal family, or else it is kept by the whaler himself, for it is the preferred delicacy. But on this night the Cook family sent me an enormous slice of the heart, ten or twelve pounds' weight of it, for my personal meal. They also sent about two hundred pounds of the steak for my men, who cooked some of it in the oven and had some of it boiled.

Whale meat cooked *kai-umu*—in the earth oven— does not much appeal to me. It is baked in a generous quantity of coconut cream; and while this is a cooking medium I can enjoy as a change, in Polynesian countries I avoid it as much as possible, finding that it tends to weary the palate. It seems to make most meats taste the same, and is really at its best with chicken or fish. A second method, *hai-haka,* or boiling, is no more attractive. I like boiled whale less than I like boiled beef; which is to say that I could accept it as nourishment, but without enthusiasm.

My portion of heart I had grilled, *kai-tunu,* to my complete satisfaction. I kept the grilling process to a minimum and had the meat sliced to a convenient beefsteak thickness, and found the meal delicious: rather like beefsteak flavoured lightly with kidney.

On the heels of these gifts, two of the successful hunters came to talk whaling with me, and brought a case of beer.

When they had gone I said to David, "They're good men. They're really good." For in the beginning of my stay they had regarded me as a competitor, to be avoided, and I had not seen them at such close quarters before.

David agreed with me. "There are no better," he said. He was silent for a while, and then he enlarged on this.

"Men who follow a hard trade; men who have a

hard trade and give their lives to it because they like it are always good, Olefi. Good men and good company."

I looked around at our own men, relaxed and cheerful in their thoroughgoing poverty after three months of frustration and failure; three months of hard work for which they had been paid nothing at all. Some of them clustered in a corner, seated on the mats and singing, and I knew that I would never in my life find better men or better friends.

At that stage I was beginning to lose my optimism; I had almost resigned myself to the thought that the season would pass and I would not get my whale. But there was one more possibility.

Tavi stopped by our house with good advice.

"Go to Hunga," he said. "At Hunga every morning there are fifty whales, right under the cliffs. From Hunga you will get your whale, and once you get it you can come and hire the fastest boats in port to tow it back. You will have no trouble at all."

I listened to Tavi with some respect, for I believed that, unlike me, he was a man who had caught his metaphorical whale. He was no Polynesian but a deceptively frail-looking Dane, with long blond hair worn down on his shoulders. Nearly everything about him was nonconforming, even his history. University training as a civil engineer had been the key to unlock the door of the South Seas for him, bringing him the friendship of influential Polynesian princes and giving him proprietorial rights in an island of his own, where he lived as he wished for the ten years that preceded our meeting, browsing green leaves and philosophy, and quite untouched by the small and violent turmoils that racked the outside world.

There was no civil engineering to distract him on Hunga Ha'apai, an otherwise uninhabited volcanic island, the most westerly of the Tongan group. There are no buildings except for a tunnel he inhabits and a cool and airy coconut-leaf shelter or two. There is not even a wharf, not even a beach on which to pull up a canoe, so that, except in the very finest weather, Tavi homing from fairly frequent travels must swim to the rocks from the schooner lying well off. Anyone who has seen such rocks in heavy weather will understand a small part of my respect for him.

He has no luggage to worry about, for he needs to take nothing with him unless it is another case of the books which are all that he asks of civilization. Hunga has a wealth of natural foods, from which Tavi selects only vegetable items, though fish and shellfish, eggs and sea birds are in such plenty as would feed an army, and the husbanding of pigs and poultry would present no problems. His diet involves him in a minimum of subsistence gardening. Most of his food grows on native bushes and trees, and he supplements this larder with bananas, pineapples, and a few vegetables such as taro.

He does this though he has no strong convictions on vegetarianism. He is not a nudist either, though on his island he goes naked. When he visits the inhabited islands of Tongatapu and Ha'apai, as he is frequently asked to do, he wears clothes, but he has no need to buy them. They are provided, rightly he feels, by the people who seek his company. He doesn't smoke, not from conviction, but because he doesn't care for smoking. He doesn't like most alcoholic drink. Good wine is an exception to this, but a bottle doesn't often come his way, and he is content to wait until it does. He is a bachelor, but he would marry the compatible girl who would follow his way of life without argument—provided he loved her. He cherishes his solitude but abandons it frequently to help others, and at times has played host to a small group of Tongan lads who have come to his island seeking coaching in mathematics.

His slight weight—125 pounds—insignificant stature and delicacy of feature seem to proclaim him an unlikely candidate for the wilderness life he successfully follows. Boyhood friends especially would have been unlikely to forecast such a future for the lad they knew as Preben Kauffmann.

Kauffmann is an Austrian name, but Tavi's father was a Danish Customs officer, so that his boyhood was always spent near the sea, in a variety of Danish ports. Never long in any place, he formed his locality attachment to the sea itself; though once again, with the consistent moderation that characterizes his beliefs, he likes to be near it rather than on it. He doesn't care for travel. His boyhood dreaming of the South Seas was tempered by the desire to create things, which led him, when he considered his future vocation, to settle first on architecture and then, with an increasing appreciation of the factors involved, on engineering, in which field appropriate construction is not a matter of whim or opinion but of mathematics.

Tavi's studies in Denmark were conducted against the background of German occupation; and when the university buildings were seized for the accommodation of troops and he was shifted to quarters that had cooking facilities he decided, in an experimental way, to try vegetarianism. After a week he was delighted with the experiment; feeding became so cheap he could afford to buy himself all kinds of luxuries: figs from Smyrna and Arabian dates and little exotic sweetmeats.

The atom bomb, when it exploded, convinced him of the futility of a life devoted to material construction and creation, and he remembered his boyhood dreams of the South Seas.

"I lost faith in European man," he told me earnestly. "On paper his philosophy is grand and beautiful, but war destroys values. I am a believer in reality. I never value money, for example. Material things are an absolute necessity for human existence, but money, especially paper money, is a kind of fiction. It's based on confidence, a confidence that everyone will live up to his obligations, but wars have proved that this confidence is misplaced, as far as Western civilization is concerned.

"When you don't have confidence in a way of life you withdraw from it. 'Stand back and let the children have their game', as they say. Then, too, I had the distressing experience that my teeth were beginning to decay, so I got out.

"I went to Sweden first, doing some research on hydraulics. Then I went to work in America, to make some money quickly, so I could buy a boat and get away. I estimated three years in America would buy me a boat that would take twelve years in Denmark or Sweden.

"You understand, I didn't want to unmask pretence, but to remove myself from where it flourished. To adopt a Tongan way of life would also be to adopt pretence, and so I don't do that. But Tongans are wise in their pretences. We like to think of ourselves as so honest, so good, so just. But a Tongan admits his faults freely. He knows what reality is, even though he doesn't live by it.

"People who have worldly possessions have to adopt pretences to protect them. This isn't easy to understand. A European is not obliged to meet requests, but his convention is that he tell the truth when he's cornered on this subject. If someone asks him for something he values he can say no. A Tongan is obliged to share all his goods with his fellows if they need them; but his conventions allow him to pretend he hasn't got them. A person who had no pretences in Tonga would have no goods either."

Tavi, sitting at ease, European-style, on one of the two benches in our house, framed against a background of vivid laughing life among the coconuts, seemed in his person to be as far removed from reality as in his

165

mind he was centred there. He wore a blue coat-shirt over the wide easy freedom of a matching *vala*, the knee-length Tongan skirt worn by men. His feet were bare; his only other item of wear being a wrist-watch. His hair was fine, silky and slightly wavy, as was his beard. He was extremely short-sighted; when he looked at a book he held it inches from his pale blue eyes.

He spoke very freely to me and did not mind the questions I asked. It may have been a long time since he had found an ear responsive to the expression of his basic philosophy.

"Don't get me wrong," he said. "I'm not in Tonga to help Tongans. And I don't want to adopt a Tongan way of life. All I want to do is live a natural life and find a peace of mind."

"Is it a natural life, then, to live alone on an island? Doesn't 'living naturally' stipulate that man should be constantly making the kind of adjustments made necessary by the presence of a partner, at least? In other words, shouldn't the 'natural man' be married?"

"Probably yes," he said. He picked up a pencil from the table and played with it, and a slight smile tugged at the corners of his delicate mouth, where the yellow beard was scanty.

"Marriage is in my philosophy, this is true. I was engaged to a girl in Denmark who professed to believe in the same things as I. But after I was two years in America it became obvious from her letters she had been hoping my ideas would change. When I taxed her with this she admitted it. That was obviously unworkable. Then, a few years ago I decided to marry a Tongan girl I had become very fond of. It was fine as far as she was concerned. I told her exactly what her position would be—she could live the way she wanted to, she could eat meat, for example, but she couldn't expect me to provide anything other than what I would provide for myself. I wouldn't alter my way of life in the slightest. I would not conform with the conventions the family followed or the habits of the community. The fact was, I had found the family was making arrangements and realized I would become a member of that family unless I made myself very clear. The matter was dropped. We are good friends."

"You haven't kept a mistress? That's what so many aliens want to do here; that's what brings a lot of them."

"I don't play games," Tavi said firmly. Since everything is known about everybody in these Friendly Islands I was already aware that he was speaking the simple truth.

In spite of Tavi's distaste for Western civilization, he had loved the clean modernity and the friendliness of San Francisco. He acquired sailing experience from his friendship with Allen Olinger, a dentist who raced a thirty-foot Hurricane class keeler, the *Hanaloa*, in San Francisco Bay. When he had his goal in financial sight Tavi found the *Hirondelle*, a 26-footer designed by Colin Archer, a double-ended Norwegian pilot-boat type that was a cruising man's dream. She had been built by a captain in the U.S. Coast Guard for a retirement trip to Hawaii, but her owner died before he could use her. Tavi bought her for less than three thousand dollars and spent eight months fitting her out.

Tavi was then thirty-seven years old. He saw an advertisement in a Quaker magazine that intrigued him. The advertiser was Harry Little, married, with a son twelve years old. He was a vegetarian who lived by subsistence gardening in Vermont, eating his crops as they came out of the ground, opposed to all preservative methods, to all food storage, to everything that tended to make his food less than perfectly fresh. Little realized that life for one of his convictions would be easier in the tropics, for there was little to sustain him

167

without storage through the long months of the Vermont winter. His life was complicated there because he had to spend so much time getting fuel for the winter and had to find money for kerosene for lighting, and woollen materials for winter clothes. So he advertised for someone to sail to the tropics and investigate the conditions for primitive living. Tavi agreed to take him to the Marquesas, and to pay his fare back from there if he found that island group unsuitable.

"After all, I would have had to do the same for hired crew," he told me, completely oblivious to Little's moral debt to him.

They were becalmed in the Horse Latitudes, and made the Marquesas fifty-four days out from San Francisco. Tavi learned his navigation as he went along. They had a raft pamphlet, as issued by the U.S. Navy. "And so I had to concentrate," he said.

Harry Little was strongly attracted by the natural conditions in the Marquesas and Tahiti that favoured his ideal life, but otherwise he saw a difficult prospect for the new settler. If they lived there they would have to take up sides, to line up on the side of the European or the native. He determined instead to go to Costa Rica and settle in the mountains there. Tavi tried hard to get him to go to Tonga, but Little was suspicious of monarchies, while for Tavi, since he had been brought up in Denmark, they seemed logical enough. In fact they had very striking advantages.

The price of land in the French Republic's colonies in Tahiti and the Marquesas was prohibitive, and there was a price on every small corner. In Tonga all land belongs to the Queen. It cannot be bought or sold, and consequently, he reasoned, it can be got without price. These persuasions had no effect upon Little, who went home, while Tavi continued alone to Tonga.

Here he immediately made several friends. A Dutch Customs officer invited him to his home. The Government agricultural officer he met there had come out to inspect a drainage scheme, and, as a direct result of this, Tavi met the Prime Minister, Prince Tungi, the heir apparent to the throne of Tonga, on his second day in the kingdom.

At that time Tonga needed a Director of Public Works, and had been unable to find a satisfactory applicant. Tavi agreed to give advice to Havea, the Minister for Public Works, on a visit to a southern island named 'Ata. 'Ata is uninhabited, though a most fertile island, and Tavi wanted to stay there. Havea said he could not, but if he served as Director of Public Works for six months he could find another island elsewhere in the Tongan groups. He stayed ten months instead of six, and in that period selected what was to become his permanent location on Hunga Ha'apai.

He already had his Polynesian name. He and Little had chosen names for themselves during their daydreaming on the voyage out, and Tavi's was the name of one of the brothers of the demi-god Maui, a brother sometimes called The Jester and sometimes The Lazy One.

Tavi is no jester, and opinion is divided as to whether the other meaning is appropriate. His meals are gathered mainly from the leaves of plants. He has tried almost everything on his island except those leaves that show a milky sap when broken: it is a safe general rule that these are poisonous. Other leaves are safe, though some of them can produce violent gastric effects. Tavi estimates that at least ten per cent of all leaves are edible, some of course being more desirable than others. The great standby is the talking tree, *puko-lea*. Each day Tavi eats about five pounds of leaves. Almost every day, too, he eats the centres of sprouted, or germinated coconuts. At that stage the nut contains a froth of fine white growth, a growth that makes a delicious salad. Very occasionally he will drink a little of the liq-

169

uid of green coconuts; more often he will use it as a cooking medium instead of water. He drinks nothing else whatever, certainly no water, his liquid requirements being provided by the leaves. He never uses coconut milk or cream because it contains too many fats. Sea-water is a standby. Combined with coconut cream and lemon juice it is a highly esteemed salad dressing in these latitudes, but Tavi uses it by itself. In an average day he will eat twelve coconuts—germinated for preference—twelve bananas, two pounds of papaw, and his green leaves. This is an expensive diet, each germinated coconut being a potential tree. To produce this wealth of food he depends not at all upon conventional agriculture.

"Sea birds are my ploughs and my horses," he told me. "They burrow deep into the ground to make their nests, and they line the burrow with dry leaves. When these are coated with manure by the young birds they make the perfect compost."

The sea birds cluster round him, using his shoulders and his head for a roost, for they have no fear of him. All the birds on his island are friends—until his visitors arrive. Tavi has few, because of the difficulties of access; but occasionally he has some Tongan lads studying with him, advancing, particularly, their mathematics. They live then as he does, except that they supplement the leafy diet with birds and birds' eggs, and fish and shellfish, all of these being legion. Tavi disapproves. The shellfish form his emergency larder, to be drawn upon when, as sometimes happens, the cyclone comes and the green leaves are destroyed.

After twelve years, how successful does he reckon his way of life to be?

"I'm happy," he said sincerely. "Prince Tungi is a good friend of mine, and that gives me the run of two libraries, Tungi's and the good collection at the palace.

I've got the friendship and the respect of all the good Tongans. But. . . . "

There was a long pause while he tailored what he had to say next. When he was committed to it he spoke quickly, very definitely:

"What I didn't realize in my attempt to live close to nature is that nature includes human nature too. It is part of the environment of human beings. The Western civilization tends to ignore the human-relations side of life. In Tonga no one will leave me alone. I am, you see, a superior tool lying around unused. You can go back to nature only as long as you can be left in nature, and as soon as other people come along you have to consider them. I've had to relinquish a worship of nature; I've had to exchange it for detachment; because human nature is an integral part of the picture of nature; and you can't worship that.

"I prize understanding above faith; faith is too primitive. Most of my solitude is devoted to the acquisition of some understanding. But there is always something that someone wants me to do, on some of the other islands. I'm building a church for Havea. It's in a remote village, but he wants it to last for a thousand years. Well, it will."

When he leaves Hunga Ha'apai on these missions Tavi uses what transport is provided. His yacht was an embarrassment: he gave it away.

"I didn't want money for it. I had to separate myself from money. When you have no money, fifty acres of coconuts is enough for fifty families and will support them well. If you sell the copra it isn't enough for one family."

In Tonga nobody laughs at Tavi, nor did I. In spite of his dissociation from the mass, his is an important place in the islands, not only because of his specialized knowledge of mathematics and engineering, but also because of the location of his home. Hunga Ha'apai is on the south-west corner of the central group of islands. When the winds come from the east it's on the leeward side of the busy internal sea passages. It is therefore a resort for those in trouble. Three times, from his residence Tavi has saved small boats and their crews from disaster. He doesn't talk about this himself, but in a nation of seamen it gets a sufficient mention.

By the time I met him I had booked my passage home. I had a clear week, no more, and at the end of that time the whaling season would have drawn to a close. There would still be some whales in the vicinity; in fact, there might be many; but in the pattern of the years they would be restless and hurrying, feeling the great emptiness of bellies they had not filled in four or five months, registering the increasing heat of the sun, the call of Antarctic water. Few whales have ever been caught in Tonga past September's end, and I could afford neither the time nor the money for wild experimentation.

We decided, all of us together, to try the ground at Hunga.

12

The wild seas would not, I think, have kept us on the beach, but there were stores to get; fuel for the launch and the completion of a refit caused by her breakdown on the night the Cooks brought in their small whale. When it was clear that we could not leave before the Monday afternoon we waited longer, and at ten o'clock or perhaps a little later we slid out of the harbour of Faua and headed for the winking light of Malinoa.

Velata carried a scratch crew, just for the journey: Ve'etutu, Maile, Olive, Finau, and myself, all of us in love with the little vessel for what she could do. The others of our crew travelled on *Kaimoana* where they could sleep protected from the rain.

Kaimoana pulled us out of harbour, but *Velata* soon settled down with the wind on her quarter and overtook the launch. Since neither of us carried lights except for a torch for signalling and as a warning to strange vessels, we were soon out of sight, a fact remarked by no one except myself, who was at the tiller. I was very well aware, of course, that we carried no compass either; we had no instruments for navigation and after we left Malinoa, eight miles out, there were no lights on our course, nor any other landmarks. The stars were no help, for the clouds obscured them.

But we had the consistency of the wind, which for days had been blowing from the south-east, the dominant wind of the monsoon, and I had no doubt that we could raise a landfall on Hunga, a tiny speck, but one no more than fifty miles away; so I said nothing but held her on the course, which would take us to a point east of the island. We intended later, if our time were good, to run out the night on the jibsail alone, carrying the wind on the port quarter and heading westerly.

But there was a scud of rain, the lights of Nuku'alofa were blotted out, and the nearer light of Malinoa dimmed alarmingly; Ve'etutu took over, turning back to relocate the launch.

I felt that even the weather fought against me; I felt that the crew and the weather in collusion would hold me from this last hope of my whale, and when the most meticulous search failed to discover the slightest sign of the launch, when by what I reckoned to be an indecisive timidity we had gone back on our tracks until the harbour once again loomed close at hand, a rising gorge persuaded me to action.

I took the helm again and headed out to sea. I held on an approximate course for four hours; approximate, because after the first hour there was nothing to give a direction except the lines of rollers, their tops breaking, their crests rising steep from narrow defiles. My companions were asleep or silent; only Maile watched the sails. Finau was huddled under a copra sack, staring at the blackness ahead. Ve'etutu was silent. I wondered whether he was asleep or composing a poem; he was a very fine poet and the sea moods triggered the kinetic phase of his artistry.

At about three in the morning he took the tiller, to my considerable relief. The moment I was unengaged I realized how tired I was. I lay down on the wet deck, covered my shoulders with a sopping sack, and in spite of the rain on my face was asleep inside the minute.

I woke just before sunrise, registering an excitement that infected the sloop. The trolling line which towed normally at our stern had made a catch, a large fish. Its method of fighting proclaimed it a Spanish mackerel, its resistance a fish of about eighty pounds. It was no sooner hooked than the shark came, his dark triangle of fin just a shade darker than the dark water, just a little way behind the white occasional wake of the fighting fish.

The shark spun wide to starboard like the rider of a water-ski, or an oropesa float at its launching, held out there a second, slid fast an equal distance to port and paused again, then with speed and surety swept in and took the mackerel behind the head, swallowing some sixty pounds of meat in a single bite bigger around than a man's chest.

In the cold of my wet awakening I didn't rise; the shark and the marlin were frequent companions of *Velata* on her hunts. I lay in the small slosh of water on the deck and listened to the Tongan words of excitement, fitting what I could of them to my small knowledge of the language. The next thing I knew, the head of the mackerel, ragged and bloody, came inboard on the hook and swept against my face. I could feel the warmth—the Spanish mackerel is one of the red-fleshed, warm-blooded fishes of the sea, a magnificent fighter on a line.

The head, from its torpedo snout to the ragged fringe of flesh below the gills, was two feet in length and a foot and a half in depth. Finau took charge of it. The mackerel, either in taking the bait or in being himself taken, had destroyed the lure, and Finau cut another strip to replace it from the amply fleshed head. That done, he cut a similar strip for himself, two and a

175

half inches wide, an inch deep, a foot long; but Ve'etutu, still on the tiller, held out a hand for it. The next went to Maile. When he cut the fourth I held out my own hand; I was fourteen hard-working hours from a meal. I was thirty years from a meal of raw fish fresh from the sea, without sauce or garnish, but the rosered quivering flesh looked good to me, and when I sank my teeth into its warmth it freshened my mouth like crisp fruit and put new heart into me. The Tongans watched me with interest; not many Westerners in their experience liked the clean sharp lively taste of any raw fish but oysters; and my obvious enjoyment delighted them. It intensified the relationship we already enjoyed. But my teeth could not, like theirs, cope with the rubber-tough skin.

While we ate the mackerel the sky lightened in the east, and with the dawn there was a break in the clouds ahead, and a great shout from Ve'etutu. The twin islands called Hunga lay so directly in our course that the most accurate of instrument-assisted calculations could not have improved our position. After that it was not quite so astonishing that *Kaimoana*, on her compass course, lay between us and the islands. She had overtaken us during the night while we eased along under the little jib alone; we must have earlier overtaken her in a seesaw after she had assumed the lead when we went back to look for her. We put on sail, rapidly overhauled her for at least the third time that night, and set in between the islands.

They lay along the rim of what had once been a circular crater about two miles in diameter, cupping it to the north-east and north-west. On the third side, to the south, a heavy break sometimes exposed a third remnant of the crater rim, a development of yellow stone almost at the surface.

Hunga Tonga, the more easterly island, was steep and high, a narrow precipitous ridge of no great bulk, though from a distance, because of its curve, it looked wider than it actually was. It seemed to offer no foothold whatever, but in the distant past some swimmers had visited it and planted coconuts at its highest point; and the lodgment of the falling fruit, so adequately protected from shock by its thick padding of coir fibre, had spread the palm to every cranny on both precipices where there was any possibility that it could be nourished.

Hunga Ha'apai, to the west, offered a kindlier prospect. The inner surface of the crater was as precipitous. But from the peak of the ridge the land spread to the west in negotiable slopes, covered with a good depth of soil, fertilized frequently and thoroughly by the screaming millions of birds that wheeled about its peaks and nested on its ledges. It was here that Tavi lived, but there was no sign of occupation; no tracks showed on the well-grassed open slopes; no construction of any sort could be seen from the sea.

In this first contact I had little time to take note of the land. We came to look for whale, and for as long as it took us to sail across the crater we were disappointed. But then we turned back, saw the signals from *Kaimoana* a mile behind tokening "whale", and got ready for the chase: set the sails, laid out the irons, uncovered the line, cleared the decks, and raced back to pick up our normal hunting crew from the launch.

Now the whales seemed to be everywhere; four or five grey balloons of whale breath drifted in to mingle with the constant fountained spray from the rocks, and at the same time, out at sea near the heavy break to the south, a young bull began leaping high in the air. Most were travelling north through the pass formed by the sunken crater; they proved urgent and restless, and we could get nowhere near them.

Meanwhile our troll lines were busy. We hauled them in when we were close in pursuit of the whales, but otherwise left them in tow, and here, among these volcanic rocks, we began to reap a harvest; all fighting fish, Spanish mackerel and queenfish, sharks and large trevally, and a yellow-striped predator I had not seen before, a fighting seven-foot length of spring-steel that snapped a heavy hook with ease and came immediately back to repeat the punishment. Among the volcanic islands the fishing is at its best, and this, but for the frustration of the larger hunt, could have been an interlude of wild delight.

But at the end of the day we were tired and disappointed, and we had gear to mend, for the winds had risen. We pulled in to an anchorage hard under the rocks of Hunga Ha'apai, a chancy anchorage, open to too much weather for safety or for comfort, with winds that switched around the high islands with fey, unpredictable velocities. Hardly was our anchor down and we immobile than a huge whale, challenging in size that enormous cow which, as I have said, was the largest humpback I have ever seen, cruised slowly between us and the rock as though he too sought shelter in the night.

In the darkness we could hear them, grunting and rumbling, emptying their lungs with a great soughing sound.

The next day was the same. We came to the end of our food and fuel for the fire, and when the chase was over for the day we prepared to go ashore. There was a place on the north-west side of Hunga Ha'apai where long fingers of rock thrust into the sea, and between these fingers there was some shelter from the cross-sweep of the sea. There was one place where the waves licked almost the top of the rim-rock, and this was the traditional landing-place.

We set out a stern-anchor and crept up to the rock. The sweep of the sea and the confining walls increased the height of the waves in this place; though the weather was calm, they lifted up and down about ten feet on the face of the rock. With the others going ashore I stripped off my clothes; the likelihood was that we would have to swim for it, or even if we came close enough, as seemed too risky to be likely, that we would miss a footing and fall back into the swirl of waters.

But David and Ve'etutu were old hands at the delicate task. With four men on sweeps and others standing to the anchor-lines, they eased in until *Velata's* bow tossed within inches of the yellow cliff. It was dangerous to a degree that I could not bear to weigh; the tender wood danced within inches of the claiming rock; the least touch would have wrecked us, and yet we swung a couple of fathoms vertically up and down the irregular face of the cliff.

The gulls that thronged the island were screaming, not frightened but curious; most of them would never have seen such a landing. They wheeled above us. Lau'ia was the first man ashore; he leapt deftly, neatly from the bow at the top of the upswing and turned to catch the tools thrown to him—axes and a shovel and large bush-knives—and the fish we were to cook in an earth oven.

Finau was second; he took the top of the cliff at a run, the bow swung low again, and he was out sight; as we came up to the crest once more we saw him, an octopus in one hand the other reaching to take a wheeling bird from the sky. The octopus, king of its rock-pool, had been unaware of any danger until Finau caught it a second only after his feet touched the island; the bird was too slow for his fingers, perhaps the air was too crowded for winged manoeuvre.

At the top of the next wave three more men leapt for the shore; I came at the next ascent, and already the line of my predecessors was scrambling up the rocks towards the verdant hillside. By the time we reached the grass Finau carried four birds and an octopus in his hand, the birds screaming like banshees, their noise lost in the great scream from the feathered air above the island.

Past the rimrock, birds were everywhere, standing by eggs that lay, in singles or in pairs, so closely together that it was impossible to avoid breaking them if you took a careless step. Bare toes were yellowed with yolk, at most moves we pushed eggs gently from the path. There were no nests, but the extreme variation in size between the larger and the smaller ends of each egg kept it from rolling more than an inch or two, even on flat rock. In a matter of moments my companions collected about a gross of the freshest eggs, and thereafter didn't disturb any. They were the size of the ordinary commercial hen eggs, certainly as these are sold in Tonga. Several of our men caught terns from the air as Finau had done. Meantime all of them set about gathering firewood for the earth oven.

Ve'etutu and I started up over the long grass-grown meadow slopes to the top of the island. Near the rocky part of the ridge there were brief spaces where no eggs lay on the ground; here, as I soon found, the grass was not negotiable by reason of its seed-pods, savagely hooked. Beyond this grass the cliff fell away in a precipice to the ocean-filled crater; and on small ledges of this precipice all kinds of birds were nesting. Great fat chicks, as large as young geese, thrust indignant bills in our direction; they were too fat and greasy to eat, so Ve'etutu assured me. They were frigate birds and boobies, and what seemed to be gannets, though somehow I did not expect to find these here in a mixed rookery and decided that my identification was wrong.

We stood on the cliff, on top of the beautiful island, and caught our breath for the sight of whales beneath; a dozen or twenty of them, cruising gently but restlessly, staying nowhere. Again, by the break, were some leaping; I have never failed to stop and marvel at the

180

power that lifts that bulk as high as a five-storey build-ing from the water.

We plunged from the rock into light tropical forest. There were several groves of coconuts and, surround-ing them, some of the wilder vegetation. Papaws grew in abundance; my naked skin was deeply wealed by their stems as I pushed through them. For the papain, the active principle of the sap which has commercial use as a meat tenderizer, produces in humans a violent reactive itch. I was the more vulnerable to it for, in this shelter of bush, everywhere that shrubs and trees took over from the grass, the soft and friable earth had been tunnelled for the deep extensive nests of the shear-waters, the mutton-birds of Tasmania and New Zea-land. The tunnels were empty; the birds would return in January or February; but at every step the ground collapsed beneath me, and I plunged as deep as my crotch into the miniature caverns. This was painful, especially when the root of a tree intercepted a plung-ing toe or knee, and it was no consolation to see Ve'etutu also thrown thus violently about, though oc-casionally it was a relief to walk in the valleys created by his falls.

We sat down near the top of the hill and ate papaws. A crab the size of a bread-and-butter plate scuttled from beneath Ve'etutu's bare haunches, and he leapt in the air with a cry. The crab, yellow like papaw skin, had probably never seen the sea; perhaps with others of his kind he was developing new habits that would result some day in a new breed of crustacean.

There were places where we saw hundreds of young coconuts set out to sprout; but this was the only sign we found that Tavi had helped nature to provide his sustenance. There was not on all that island any sign of a track that would have assisted his movements from place to place; perhaps his light build saved him from the erratic plunging into the depths of earth that made my progress a minor misery. We did not go to the crest where he had tunnelled through for a living-place; that was his private domain and we did not approach it.

But the papaws would have flourished greatly if the shadowing branches overhead had been a little trimmed; the taro we saw planted at random in the shade would have returned a better dividend for an allowance of open air and sunshine. Healthier roots and fruits would have made healthier eating, I thought; and I realized that Tavi, though he had achieved the fantasy of his Crusoe island, was missing out between the theory and the practice of his beliefs.

There was no perfection here on Hunga. There could not even be the spurious perfection of an individual, complete and non-competitive exploitation of nature's wealth. For the rats had moved in. They had nibbled the best of most of the ripe papaws on the tree; they had eaten thousands of the eggs that Tavi left untouched and had killed thousands of the chicks. They would kill some of the trees; and perhaps, in a few generations, they would lay the island waste and set an ugly seal upon the certainty of their own destruction.

Tavi too had lost his whale. He had failed to catch it —this, at least, I believed. I was sad for him, and a little for myself, as I went back to the earth oven.

We had been away some hours, and the cooking was in progress. Thirty or forty coconuts had been gathered and the milk expressed to make a baking medium for the fish and some birds. The eggs had already been baked in hot sand. Most of the captured birds had been grilled and already eaten; these were titbits only, not for the rest of the week's eating.

The island birds were still in uproar; they wheeled far out where *Velata* and *Kaimoana* lay in the bay.

Lau'ia had found, cast up on the shore rocks, a varnished water barrel, brass-bound and nearly new, from the wreckage of some sleek yacht; *Diablo*, perhaps,

182

though the keg must have travelled far and fast from that. Beneath the overhang of cliffs were pools of fresh water at which it could be filled, and I went to attend to this myself. I left the barrel soaking in the pool when it was filled, for in the sunshine its staves had begun to lift apart.

Farther to the edge of the sea the pools were salt, and here they were filled with life; small and lovely fish, brilliant in fantastic livery, centred every one, unafraid of my shadow or my reflection. I watched an Emperor Angelfish, perhaps a third grown at six inches long. It had zebra stripes in white and smoky blue on black, an exquisitely sculptured, meticulously painted extravagance of form. Its pool seemed to be above the high tide, and I wondered how, when it came to its full size, it would manage to live there.

But each pool had its lonely king, its Tavi; and each, no doubt, when time was up, its escape route through the storms or the king tides to the open sea. At certain levels of the rock, where the waves coursed through, the chocolate cowries fed in large droves, no two the same, each beautiful in its patterns.

The following day we chased whales again. I had little heart in it now, for I had little belief in our success. On Friday came our last chance, and for an hour or more hope came close, as we turned and twisted to chase a pod of young bulls, light-hearted small monsters of forty feet or so, seeming to play with us, deliberately allowing us to come within ten yards or so of their tails, swimming ahead at just our speed, just at the surface, joyful in the wild wind that quickened their senses, I thought, as much as ours.

We turned aside twice, once to launch an unsuccessful harpoon at the largest turtle I have ever seen, a monster that seemed seven feet long at least; it may have been a leatherback. The other time we turned to another small whale haunting the rocks near Hunga

Tonga; it appeared only once and we came back to the pod.

We were getting no nearer, and David gave a sudden order. We swung about and headed for Nuku'alofa. Our whaling season was over, and we were resigned to failure.

Ve'etutu and I, with a few of the others, switched to *Kaimoana*, to go back under power. I went to join him in the wheelhouse, but he was curt with me.

"You get to the stern, Olefi. Get a line out, and catch a fish to give the Queen."

I tried, and for a while, rolling on our way, we haunted the rocks, but I had no success. I went into the wheelhouse after a couple of hours and Ve'etutu turned on me angrily.

"Get back there. I'll take you where you'll get a fish."

He swung *Kaimoana* to the big break, where heavy seas were leaping to the half-tide rock that was the third remnant of the ancient volcano. The wallowing launch came into the break so close it fell away, with receding seas, from the rock, and wallowed on. I could have leapt for the yellow stone and made it. A moment later my hooks were over the spot. I took two fish, one on each of my lines, within three seconds of each other; and I was reminded of the two koango I had taken the first time I had fished for Queen Salote. These were not koango, they were a larger variety, each running about thirty pounds in weight.

I coiled up my lines and went to the wheelhouse.

"Well, I got a fish for the Queen," I said, and Ve'etutu answered shortly, "Yes". I looked at him sharply, and there was a tear running from the corner of his eye into his beard.

That was the end of it. It was not for me in that place in that year to catch a whale, but I tried. And in the total event I became possessed of something much

184

greater: the friendship of fine men, and a closer under-standing. I know what it feels like to hold to a whale; it feels strong and fine, and the strength and the goodness come from the communion of effort. I know what it feels like to lose the game; and it is not important.

The record is one of failure, but it was a strengthen-ing season, for the spirit's atrophy is not engendered in the kinetics of even unsuccessful effort; nor does it come with the cessation of a search to which a man and his companions have been fully and honestly com-mitted.

I think I grew a little in the good comradeship of men, and my gain was more enduring than my goal.

New TOWER Books
of Exceptional Interest

New TOWER Books
of Exceptional Interest

NEW PUBLIC AFFAIRS BOOKS FROM TOWER

TIME IS SHORT

AND THE

WATER RISES

John Walsh, with Robert Gannon

Vivid, true-life account of the struggle to save
10,000 doomed animals from a flooded South
American rain forest. Recommended by the World
Wildlife Fund.

Tower   T-095-9   95¢

A Tower Natural Heritage Book

Please allow 3 weeks for filling orders.

Tower Publications, Inc., 185 Madison Ave.
New York, N. Y. 10016

Please send me the books circled above.

Amount enclosed $............(Please add 15¢ per book for handling and postage.)

ORDER BY BOOK # ONLY
CIRCLE THE NUMBER OF BOOKS WANTED

In the event we are out of stock of any of your choices, please underline the alternative *numbers*.

Name ....
(Please print.)

Address ....

City..................... State.......... Zip..........

Send check, cash, or money order—*NO STAMPS PLEASE.*
CANADA ONLY—Add 10¢ for every Canadian dollar order.